EVERTON NUMBER 9

Nine Players. One Iconic Shirt

Jim Keoghan

INTRODUCTION

There is something about Everton and that 'Number 9' shirt. Throughout the club's long history, so many of our heroes, the players who have often come to define an era or a side have worn that number on their backs.

The names run like a panoply of Goodison greats, names like Dean, Hickson, Gray and Ferguson, players whose exploits have become an indelible part of the club's grand narrative.

And these greats have tended, with one notable exception, to inhabit a 'type'; big, strong, unyielding; the kind of players who leave their opponents black and blue the following day. The Everton 'Number 9' has almost become a useful shorthand, a term that immediately conjures up a certain kind of footballer, the kind that would charge through a melee of players to meet a cross with an unstoppable header.

For a club that likes to pride itself on the commitment to a style of football imbued with skill and grace, the classic Everton 'Number 9' is something of an incongruous presence, sitting uneasily amongst the ranks of the School of Science. But that is to ignore something else about Evertonians, the desire to see players die for the shirt. As much as the exponents of pass-and-move are appreciated, the fans also value tenacity, the desire to go above and beyond in the name of the cause. And that's what these players tended to represent, this desire made flesh, that elemental part of what it is to be a Blue.

Although that's not to say that they were mere battering rams. There was more to these players than that. Each, despite their ability to put their heads in places others feared to tread, had more to their arsenal than just tenacity. They were skilful footballers, blessed with attributes rooted in Everton's grand traditions. They could not have achieved the feats they did via brute force alone.

It's telling that today, in an age when shirt numbers mean nothing anymore, the era of the expanded squad reducing the positional familiarity of the old 1-11, Everton's 'Number 9' still retains its power. It is still given frequently to the player who is expected to lead the line, the one number in the first eleven that keeps its roots in the past.

Its most recent incumbent is Dominic Calvert Lewin, a player who embodies all the attributes of his more famous forbears; strong, physical, great in the air. 'DCL' has talked at length about the responsibility he has felt in donning the shirt, the expectation that comes with it. And that's understandable. With a tradition that stretches back to the great Dixie Dean, it has retained its power as few others have.

This short book, exploring the lives of nine of those figures aims to illustrate why that is the case, to show just what they gave to this club. It's not an exhaustive exploration and nor does it cover everyone who has ever worn that number, but it is a collection of the greats, the lions of Goodison who have helped make the 'Number 9' what it is.

UTFT

CHAPTERS

WILLIAM RALPH 'DIXIE' DEAN

(433 appearances, 383 goals)

Back in the 1920s, Everton were in dire need of inspiration. After the break-up of the club's title-winning pre-war side, a rebuilding process was being undertaken. But progress was patchy and with the club mired in mediocrity, something more was needed.

The club's secretary-manager, Tom McIntosh, set out to hunt for that 'something more'. Luckily, he didn't have too far to look.

William Ralph 'Dixie' Dean, a young forward from Birkenhead, had been turning heads with his startling form at Tranmere Rovers during his short time with the Wirral club. In his first full season at Prenton Park, Dean found the back of the net 27 times in just 27 appearances. Along with attention from Everton, he was soon attracting interest from a wealth of other top-flight clubs, including Arsenal, Newcastle United and Liverpool.

But where would he go? The answer arrived on Monday 16 March 1925: the day that Dean of Prenton Park became Dean of Goodison.

'One afternoon,' the man himself said in an interview with the sports writer John Roberts years later, 'I cleared off to the pictures and when I got home my mother told me Mr. McIntosh from Everton had been and was waiting for me at the Woodside Hotel. I ran the two and a half miles there. I couldn't get there quick enough. Mr. McIntosh asked me did I want to play for Everton, and that was that.'

Dean didn't even ask how much he was getting paid. He simply said yes, grasping the dream of playing for his boyhood club.

He was signed for £3,000, no small amount to splash out on a teenager by the standards of the time. But his potential was widely understood. For Everton, a side struggling to recapture its pre-war form, his promise of potency was worth the outlay.

Aware of the pressure the fee might place on the teenager, the *Liverpool Daily Post and Mercury* pleaded for patience, saying, 'It is probably the heaviest transfer fee that has ever been paid for a mere boy. ... It is to be hoped the crowd will not make a "god" of Dean. He is very human and has many boy-like touches.'

Except he didn't look 'boy like' for very long. After a haltering start, as the youngster found his feet, Dean quickly became the goal-scoring machine that Everton needed. By the close of the 1925/26 campaign, his first full season with the club, the cry of 'Give it to Dixie' would ring out around Goodison whenever Everton had the ball, so devastating had he become.

There are competing theories as to how he became

'Dixie'. For a long time, it was assumed to be a reference to his dark complexion, his likeness to someone from the USA's deep south (Dixieland). But more recently, it was suggested by Tranmere Rovers club historian, Gilbert Upton that it was a corruption of his childhood nickname, 'Digsy' (acquired from his approach to the children's game of tic, where Dean would dig his fist into the backs of others [hence 'Digsy']).

Whatever the truth, by the end of that inaugural campaign, 'Dixie's' 33 goals had quickly made that £3,000 transfer fee appear a bargain. And yet, the optimism that surrounded this new hero was very nearly brought to an abrupt end in June 1926 when Dean suffered a dramatic brush with death.

A motorbike crash in North Wales resulted in the young forward suffering a fractured skull, a broken jaw, eye injuries and a concussion. He was unconscious for 36 hours and initially, it was thought he could die. And even when that possibility had receded, there were still fears that he might not play again, robbing Everton of one of its stellar talents before his career had even got going.

But fortune smiled on the Everton cause for once. Dean recovered. He was back playing for Everton within four months. Although the recovery was not as quick as Dean had liked, from a medical perspective it was exceptionally fast. On his return, away against Leeds United at Elland Road, any fears about the accident's long-term effects quickly receded when, in typical Dean style, he powered home a header from a corner.

Dean's almost superhuman ability in the air during his career gave rise to a peculiar and long-held rumour after the crash, that his heading ability had been augmented by metal plates inserted into his forehead while in hospital. But it was an apocryphal tale. The metal plates in question had been inserted in his jaw and then removed when the bone had set. It was a good story though, one that appeared to make more sense than the mundane reality, that his Godlike ability in the air was simply down to practice and hard work.

Upon recovery, Dean continued to score freely, gradually establishing himself as one of the most prolific attacking players in the country. But as yet, the Everton team that surrounded him was failing to reach his lofty standards. That changed in the 1927/28 campaign, a season that would cement Dean's legacy as not just an Everton legend but also one of the greatest forwards to ever play the game.

As part of the rebuilding process occurring at the club, Everton had recruited the talented outside-right, Ted Critchley in the summer. With Alec Troup on the left, the Blues now had two gifted providers on either wing, two players who could provide the kind of ammunition that Dean craved. It was a partnership that would yield spectacular dividends.

Dean's form that season was simply mesmerising. By November, with Everton top of the league, the colossus of Goodison had played 15 games and found the net 27 times, including hat-tricks against Portsmouth, Leicester City and Manchester United.

Tentatively, Dean had his sights on the English goalscoring record, which had recently been set by George Camsell of Middlesbrough, who had scored 59 goals during the 1926/27 campaign (albeit in the second tier). With just over a third of the season gone, he was nearly half-way there.

Over the months that followed, Everton remained in the hunt for the title, and the man himself closed in on Camsell. By late March, after bagging a brace in a 2–2 draw against Derby County, he reached 45, claiming the record for most goals in a First Division season (previously held by Ted Harper of Blackburn Rovers).

As the season closed, both the club and Dean (although he slightly less so) were still well-positioned to claim their respective titles. In the league, with three games to go, it was a head-to-head battle between Everton and Huddersfield Town for the title. And in the goalscoring stakes, Dean needed nine more goals to beat Camsell's record. For Everton's unstoppable centre-forward, it was a tough proposition but not one beyond his skills.

Dean got two in a 3–2 win over Aston Villa and then followed this with four in a 5–3 victory over Burnley. At the same time, Everton pushed further ahead of Huddersfield and, after the Yorkshiremen lost their penultimate match of the season, the title was Goodison bound.

The presenting of the trophy would have been exciting enough for Evertonians. After all, it was the first time in over a decade that the club had won any silverware. But there was also the issue of Dean's record to consider. Three more goals were needed to best Camsell, and there was just the one game left to do it.

But would the great man play?

Towards the end of the Burnley game, Dean had sprained a leg muscle and limped off. With Saturday approaching and the leg continuing to give him discomfort, Everton's trainer/physio Harry Cooke sprang into action.

'From the Wednesday night until the Friday, he was with me at home, my home in Alderley Avenue, Birkenhead,' Dean told John Roberts. 'Old Harry kept putting clay plasters on [the muscle] until the Friday night, even leaving one on overnight as well. Old Harry cured it, and on the Saturday, of course I was fit.'

On the day itself, although the official attendance was said to be just under 49,000, it's thought that around 60,000 (nervous) Blues crammed into Goodison to witness history being made.

Did the man himself share those nerves? As he did before every home game, Dean caught the number 44 tram from Water Street, got off, and walked along Goodison Road, chatting all the time to fellow fans. He was relaxed, motivated and, as he revealed to John Keith in *Dixie Dean: The Inside Story of a Football Icon*, confident in his abilities:

'I needed three goals against Arsenal, who were the greatest club in the land. But that didn't worry me whatsoever. I always used to think, "I'm better than you."'

Despite Arsenal taking a quick lead on the two-minute mark, the hopes of the fans were given a huge boost almost immediately after, when Dean opened his account with a typically powerful header.

Not long after Arsenal had restarted proceedings, the man himself was then brought down in the box. Penalty to Everton! There was only one person to take it. Goodison held its breath.

'I intended to place the penalty in the corner,'

he later recalled. 'Instead, it went in-between the keeper's legs. It wasn't one of my better kicks.'

Not that it mattered. Camsell's record had been equalled. And, with most of the game remaining, Dean needed only one more to nudge out in front.

As the crowd waited for him to strike again, Arsenal levelled. With the title secured and that scoring record exercising minds, it was one of those rare occasions at Goodison when the opposition's efforts to secure victory hardly mattered.

What was of more concern to the increasingly agitated crowd as the minutes ticked along was the growing impregnability of the Gunners' defence, which seemed determined to spoil the day. No matter what Everton threw at it, the back line remained resolute.

And then, with around four minutes left, Everton won a corner. Troup trotted out to take it. 'As the ball came in' reported the *Football Express* 'Dean was in the midst of a bunch of players – friend and foe, and when it was a case of whose head was going to reach the ball first, it was a foregone conclusion it would be Dean's. He nodded the ball into the right-hand corner of the net.'

Goodison exploded. It was a noise so loud, so the legend goes, that it sent the pigeons around the Pier

Head scattering off into the sky.

The remaining minutes of the match passed by in a deafening whirl of noise as the crowd sang and cheered without pause. When the end came, the pitch was flooded with Blues eager to celebrate not just the club's first title win that decade but also the remarkable achievement of their beloved centre-forward.

Not that they would find Dean. Just prior to the game's conclusion, the hero of the hour had already made a quiet exit, as he later confided to John Roberts: 'I turned round to the referee and I said: "Look, I'm going off, if you don't mind, tell them I'm going off for a 'Jimmy' or something." And he said: "Listen, if I were you I'd be in there now." I went off, and that was that, because I would have got murdered.'

Although Everton had much to thank Dean for, possessing a talent such as his did not come risk-free for the Blues. During the 'Dixieland' era, there frequently existed two different and wildly contrasting versions of Everton. There was the side led by the talismanic Dean, which was capable of laying waste to all comers. And then there was the side that played without Dean, which often struggled, so over-dependent was it on him.

The cost of this over-dependence had been felt immediately after that title-winning campaign when

an injury-troubled couple of seasons for their dominant centre-forward had seen Everton struggle and
eventually drop into the second tier – the first time
that had ever happened to the club. Everton had
powered back immediately, but, once again had only
done so with Dean fit and leading by example.

But with a few additions to the squad, most notably
the Manchester City forward, Tommy Johnson, the
side that would eventually start life back in the First
Division is widely regarded as the most complete of
the 'Dixieland' era, one that would go on to claim the
title at the first time of trying.

With Dean as the focal point, the Blues scored freely,
finding the net on 116 occasions (a higher figure than
in the breath-taking 1927/28 campaign). But, importantly, they were less reliant on their captain. In
the previous title-winning season, Troup had come
closest to Dean in the scoring stakes with ten goals
(50 fewer than Dixie). In the 1931/32 campaign,
Johnson chipped in with 22 and Tommy White with
18. These two complemented Dean's more modest
(yet still hugely impressive) 45.

In the following season, although the club's title
defence floundered, with Everton finishing a disappointing eleventh, the Blues made it all the way to
Wembley in the FA Cup, where they met Manchester City. Until then, shirt numbering in football had
been uncommon and largely frowned upon by the

FA. But, on that afternoon in late-April, it allowed an experiment, with both sides numbered; Everton wearing 1-11 and City 12-22. This would mean that Dean, who took number nine, became the first Everton player to wear that shirt. And he did it justice, scoring the second in Everton's 3-0 victory.

And yet, that success would prove to be the end of Dean's trophy gathering adventures at Everton. In the years that followed, final positions in the table began to tumble and the days of bringing home silverware faded away. The completeness of the 1931/32 title-winning side proved to be an aberration, meaning that the over-reliance on Dean came back to haunt Everton. Although always a threat when fit, injuries continued to limit his availability. And without him, the Blues were mediocre at best.

But it was an over-reliance that had a shelf-life. Inevitably, the closure of 'Dixieland' would always have happened at some point, likely hastened by the tolls that injuries were taking on Dean's body. Although as his 30s approached he remained a world-beater on his day, those days were becoming less frequent.

But two factors ensured a premature end to his time at Goodison.

The first of these was the appointment of Theo Kelly as club secretary. The two never got on. Dean thought Kelly dictatorial and Kelly saw Dean as an impediment to his plans to modernise the squad, his attempt to shake-off the mediocrity that had beset the club in the mid-1930s.

Without an alternative to Dean, Kelly's hand would have been weakened. Unfortunately for the club's captain, Kelly had been able to source just such an option when the young forward, Tommy Lawton was signed from Burnley in January 1937. Even Dean himself understood that Lawton had been bought as his replacement. To a lesser man, the possibility of petty jealousy might have arisen from the signing. After being the dominant force at Goodison for so long, it would naturally have hurt to see a young player bought to take his place. But Dean wasn't like that.

So the story goes, on entering the dressing room for the first time, Lawton asked Joe Mercer, 'Where's Dixie, then?', so eager was he to meet his idol.

Almost on cue, the dressing-room door burst open 'I'm here,' announced an unshaven Dean. Marching over to the young arrival, he shook his hand vigorously. Then, his arm around Lawton's shoulders, he took him to one side. 'I know you're here to take my place,' he said. 'Anything I can do to help you I will. I promise, anything at all.'

And he did. As Gordon Watson, who played left half for Everton at the time, later recalled:

'Lawton and Dean used to work together under the main stand, Dean throwing up a large cased ball, stuffed with wet paper to make it as heavy as a medicine ball.'

With such a tutor on hand, it was no surprise that Lawton quickly adapted to life at Goodison. And by the beginning of the 1937/38 season, Kelly finally had his alternative to Dean ready to take the next step. Three matches in, Kelly felt emboldened to do what would have once seemed unthinkable. Dean was dropped. He barely featured again and spent much of the remainder of his time with Everton in the reserves.

His last game in a blue shirt came in the Liverpool Senior Cup semi-final against South Liverpool at Holly Park in March 1938. Thousands turned up to see Dean play (proving his continued 'box office' appeal). Although not at his best, he still found the net, scoring the final goal in Everton's 4–1 victory.

A few days later, fans and the football world alike were stunned when it was announced that Everton's legendary centre-forward had been sold to Notts County. Neatly, from Kelly's perspective, the fee was £3,000, the same amount as Everton had paid Tranmere Rovers for the young forward all those years ago.

Dean's time in Nottingham proved to be brief, and after just nine games and a handful of goals he moved on. From there, he crossed the Irish Sea and spent some time with Sligo Rovers, helping them to a runners-up position in the league and success in the Irish FA Cup Final.

Following his Irish adventure, Dean returned to Merseyside in the summer of 1939 after being offered a lucrative contract by Hurst FC (now Ashton United). But, despite putting in a few performances for the ambitious non-league club, the outbreak of war in September 1939 would prematurely bring the curtain down on his professional playing career. Following brief stints working in an abattoir and for the local munitions manufacturer Fawcett, Preston and Co, Dean eventually enlisted with the British Army in 1940, serving on the home front.

When hostilities ceased, he began running the Dublin Packet pub in Chester (occasionally turning out for the Northgate Brewery football team). He stayed there until the early-1960s, leaving the pub trade to eventually end up, at the invitation of John Moores, working for Littlewoods as a caretaker/watchman, first in Birkenhead and later in Liverpool.

Dean passed away on 1 March 1980, age 73, after suffering a heart attack during a Derby game at Goodison. It was fitting, from one perspective, that it happened at the ground where he had made his name. This was the place forever associated with Dean, arguably the greatest Everton player to ever grace its turf.

Dean's feats for the club have echoed down the generations. But, as impressive as the figures are, 383 goals for Everton in 433 appearances, they fail to tell the full story. Dean *was* Everton during the late 1920s and 1930s. He was a player who revived the fortunes of an ailing giant, hauling it out of its post-war doldrums, restoring it to the pinnacle of the game. A colossus of a man who made Everton a force to be reckoned with once again.

TOMMY LAWTON

(95 appearances, 70 goals)

'Good luck to you. But you'll never be as good as Dixie.'

It might have been a throwaway comment, but the bus conductor who guided 17-year-old Tommy Lawton on his first trip to Goodison Park, and who saw him off with that parting shot, summed up what many Evertonians felt (or feared). The teenage prodigy, bought for £6,500 from Burnley (a huge sum for someone so young), had big shoes to fill.

Lawton was born in Farnworth, Bolton on 6th October 1919. As many young football-mad boys of the time did, Lawton grew up idolising Dean. Although he never saw his hero play, he quickly turned into something like a mini-Dean at junior level, scoring 560 goals in three years of schoolboy football, including a couple at Goodison when he turned out for Bolton schoolboys (losing 3-2 to their Liverpool counterparts).

His goalscoring exploits brought him to the notice of several Lancashire clubs. Of these, Burnley were the ones who captured his signature. Lawton made his professional debut for the Clarets against Spurs aged 17, banging in a hat-trick in the process. A few months on, 25 appearances and 16 goals to his name, he was at Everton, a big-money fee hanging over his head, and training with his idol.

Tall, slim and with slicked-back, brilliantined hair, Lawton had the makings of the perfect centre-forward. Quick and good in the air, he also possessed a hard, accurate shot, which had been honed at Turf Moor. It was one that adhered to the principle of 'low and hard' – struck with unwavering accuracy.

But, despite his many attributes, during Lawton's early time at Goodison, Dean was still the focal point of Everton's forward line, leaving the young lad from Farnworth initially consigned to the fringes, spending most of his time in the reserves. While frustrating, Lawton did not rest on his laurels as he waited for his chance, grasping the opportunity to learn from the best after taking up Dean's offer of tutelage.

'Tommy often came to me for advice and he always took notice. I liked Tommy very much' Dean said, in old age.

But just as Dean was not your average teacher, Lawton was not your average student. He had a strong work ethic, developed during his time as an apprentice at Turf Moor. There, Lawton had practised unrelentingly, aiming shots at the Bs in beer-advertisement hoardings; a level of dedication that helped him develop into one of the cleanest strikers of the ball in the English game.

After biding his time, the young forward's earliest

chance to shine in the first team came in an away fixture against Wolves in February 1937 (Dean was being rested for an upcoming FA Cup tie). On a boggy pitch, Everton were battered 7–2. Although the debutant did manage to get on the scoresheet (via a penalty), it was hardly the most auspicious of starts.

Dropped for the subsequent cup game against Spurs, his cause for future inclusion was given a boost after another lacklustre performance by the first team, one in which Everton had gained an undeserved 1–1 draw and ended the match fighting with the opposition. The directors demanded change, and, in the replay, 'master' and 'apprentice' took to the pitch for the first time, with Lawton playing outside-left.

In a match that Everton had led 3–1 at one point (only to end up losing 4–3), Lawton impressed from the off. He got his second senior goal when he put the Blues one ahead with a shot that 'Bee' in the *Liverpool Echo* described as 'so hot and fast, so rushing that the goalkeeper saw nothing of it'.

On seeing the back of the net rippling, it was said that Dean turned to Everton's left-half, Joe Mercer: 'Well, that's it' he told his teammate, 'that's the swansong, that's the end of it.' The 'master' had seen the writing on the wall. The time of the 'apprentice' was clearly at hand.

It would take a few more months before Kelly made

his definitive move but by the beginning of the 1937/38 season, it was clear the apprentice's time had come. With Everton losing the first three games of the season, during which Dean had led the line, the club's talismanic captain was dropped. In his place came Lawton.

To say he seized the opportunity provided would be an understatement. The Blue's teenage sensation ended the season as the league's top scorer with 28 goals. Along the way, he even found time to become the youngest player to score in a Merseyside derby, when he smashed in the winner from the penalty spot in Everton's 2–1 victory over Liverpool at Anfield.

But, despite thriving on the pitch, his teammates were always keen to ensure that the young striker did not let success go to his head. After another productive Saturday afternoon early on in the 1937/38 season, Lawton leisurely strolled into the dressing room the following Monday, hailing his teammates with a cocky 'morning boys'.

The greeting was met with a stretching silence. On asking what was wrong, Dean, who was in his last season with the club, spoke up: 'Who the hell do you think you are with your "morning, boys"? Who're you calling "boys"?' Dean asked all the internationals in the room to stand up and went around pointing out how many caps each had won, contrasting it all with Lawton's lack of experience.

Chastened, when Lawton went into the dressing room the next morning, he said nothing, keeping his head down. 'Not good enough for you today, then?' Dean growled. Lawton exploded in anger, telling his teammates where to go.

'Next, they'd grabbed me' he later recalled 'and thrown me up in the air. My behind hit the ceiling, I came down in about four feet of cold water. "Now you're initiated." They laughed. "Now you're a true Evertonian!" I soon learned what I could say and what I couldn't, to have respect for the top players in the game and not fancy myself too much.'

Despite his tender years, by the season's end, Lawton had quickly established himself as one of the leading talents in England.

'If Lawton is not the best centre-forward playing today,' wrote the *Sporting Star* 'I have yet to see one better ... he is not merely a proposition, but a ready-made player.'

A powerfully built six-footer, boasting the physical strength expected of a big centre-forward, Lawton was not just an accomplished striker of the ball but had become deadly in the air too. Like his beloved hero, he developed a sense of timing that was almost supernatural. It made him the stuff of defenders' nightmares, an aerial presence against whom it was at times impossible to play against.

But there was more to his game than those attributes of the classic 'battering ram' which so commonly populated English football during the inter-war years. Surprisingly nimble, he moved with grace and speed, often pouncing with a sudden burst of pace to score goals from situations where no threat had appeared to be. There was a cleverness to his play that elevated him, putting him a cut-above the other forwards who clamoured to be the country's best.

But in those early days at Everton, he did not yet have a team to match his prodigious talent. The 1937/38 season had been a frustrating one for the Blues. Although the team had scored freely, they had ended the campaign just three points off 'the drop'.

Everton were a young side and unquestionably one in transition, which perhaps contributed to their underwhelming season. But a change was on its way. In the summer of 1938, the team participated in a tournament at Ibrox, which meant a month away together in Scotland. As Lawton later wrote in his autobiography, *When the Cheering Stopped*, it was a transformative period:

'We began to know each other as people, not just players. People with different personalities, faults, varying moods, likes and dislikes...a wonderful blend developed between the players, which resulted in a far closer team spirit.'

Together with this closer sense of unity, there were other changes to the side. The mercurial yet gifted winger, Torry Gillick became a regular. The energetic and determined inside-right, Stan Bentham graduated into the first team. And Tommy Watson, who had been with the club since 1933, would gradually make the role of 'twelfth man' his own, providing vital utility cover for the side.

Everton started the 1938/39 season well, winning the opening six games (including an away victory at champions Arsenal). The club was flying high:

'I know it is early to talk and much may happen before the end of the season draws nigh, but I am much more hopeful than I was this time last year,' wrote 'Stork' in the *Liverpool Echo*, capturing the mood of the time.

With the prolific Lawton leading the line, Everton were one of a small number talked of as possible title contenders. But the expectation of any club grasping that mantle was shrouded in doubt. The prospect of war with Germany again loomed in Europe, as Nazi expansionism threatened the uneasy peace that had existed since 1918.

Prime Minister Neville Chamberlain might have secured a peace deal from Hitler at Munich towards the end of September, but there remained anxiety in many circles that war, at some stage soon, still seemed inevitable.

As it was, the season continued under this shadow and Everton remained in the hunt. The side, although less dominant than had been the case in those opening weeks, had improved dramatically compared with the previous campaign. And Lawton led by example. Everton's in-form front man would finish the campaign as the division's top scorer once again.

After a slight wobble around Christmas, Everton got back to winning ways and, following a 3–0 victory at Anfield in February, they topped the table – a position that the club never looked like giving up.

While others faltered, Everton were imperious. As the finishing line approached, the Blues had lost only one league match in 1939 (to their title rivals Wolves).

'Everton's success is a triumph of pure football ability,' wrote 'Ranger' in the *Liverpool Echo*. 'Whenever they have appeared they have won praise by their craft and artistry. After their visit to Highbury early in the season, the Arsenal programme the following week went into eulogies about them. The same thing has happened elsewhere several times.'

The Blues were eventually crowned champions in late April, finishing four points ahead of their nearest rivals, Wolves. It was a moment of optimism at Goodison. Not only were Everton champions again, but with a young side and the most gifted centre-forward in the country, theoretically, a bright future beckoned.

And yet, although the Blues would 'technically' remain the title holders for several years to follow, it was not in the way anyone would have hoped. As had been the case when Everton had won the league in 1914, conflict changed everything. Although the 1939/40 season was permitted to begin in late August, just a few weeks into the campaign the political climate darkened considerably. In early September, after the Nazis had invaded Poland, the UK and France declared war on Germany. With the country at war, the FA and the Football League cancelled what was left of the season. Everton's momentum was halted.

'They were a bloody good side,' a frustrated Lawton later wrote, 'and the next year we should have won the league again, the FA Cup and the bloody Boat Race if they'd put us in it.'

During the war, Lawton, along with several other leading footballers, was invited by the British Army to become a Physical Training instructor. Fortunately, his posting to Birkenhead meant he was able to continue making regular appearances for Everton, together with the British Army team and his Area Command side. Like many other professional players, he also made guest appearances for several other clubs during the war years, including Aldershot, Greenock Morton and Leicester City.

Although a good proportion of his professional career had been lost to the conflict, as life returned to something like normalcy after peace was declared, Lawton, still only aged 26, was about to enter his prime as a footballer and should have represented a vital asset to the Blues as the club began to adjust to the post-war footballing world. But he would not play again for Everton. Before a ball had even been kicked in the 1946/7 season, the club's stellar centre-forward had been sold to Chelsea for £11,500.

Mystery surrounded the move until Lawton's final years when he finally revealed his motivations; a transfer that had nothing to do with football. Back in 1941, Lawton had married a local girl, Rosaleen Kavanagh. When he made the move south, she declined to go accompany him.

'The marriage just wasn't working out, in fact, it was purgatory,' he later said. 'Home was hell, something had to be done.'

Although he thrived during his sole full season at

Stamford Bridge, his career took a strange turn when a souring of his relationship with his new employers resulted in him making the surprise move to Third Division South Notts County for a then-record fee of £20,000.

The transfer was the result of a promise he had made with County's recently appointed manager, Arthur Strollery, his former masseur and friend at Chelsea. Lawton had previously told Strollery that if the opportunity ever arose, he was prepared to sign for him. With his time at Stamford Bridge at an end, several clubs were interested in the star forward. But in turn, he was only interested in one.

Although he thrived at Meadow Lane, rumours of a transfer back to the big time constantly surrounded Lawton. But it would not occur until 1953, by which time he was 34 and nearing the end of his career. He'd moved to Brentford in 1952 and looked to be seeing out his career at Griffin Park when Arsenal came calling, then the reigning champions.

Frustratingly for Lawton, his move to Highbury never hit the heights he might have hoped. It was six months before he scored his first league goal and his place in the first team was rarely secure. Yet, he was able to take on the role that Dixie Dean had once provided him, that of the aging sage to the club's array of young strikers.

After Arsenal, Lawton went into management, first becoming player/manager at Kettering Town in the Southern League and then moving to Notts County. There, he lasted just one season after taking the Magpies down to the third division, receiving the blame for a relegation that was as much to do with the club's financial limitations as it was his own managerial shortcomings.

A combination of bad luck and poor decision-making characterised Lawton's post-football life as time and time again new careers or business ventures came to nothing. Life was tough and money problems haunted him for years. There were even a couple of run-ins with the law, as Lawton attempted to find increasingly desperate ways to make a living.

He was helped at times by his former clubs, with both Everton and Brentford organising testimonial matches to provide him with some kind of income. But it wasn't until the *Nottingham Evening Post* offered him a job as a football columnist in the mid-1980s, that the money troubles relented.

When judging his impact at Goodison it's useful to not just look at the goals he provided and that valuable piece of silverware he helped bring home, but to also consider what his absence meant for the club. After the war, shorn of talents such as Lawton and Mercer, Everton declined sharply. Like was not replaced by like and the inevitable result was disaster. Deteriorating form led eventually, humiliatingly, to relegation. The club ended the 1950/51 season bottom of the First Division, consigning the Blues to their second spell in the second tier.

How the club could have benefited during this time from a forward of Lawton's talents. Instead, he remains one of Goodison's great 'what ifs?'. Imagine what his legacy could have been had the war and a troubled marriage not intervened.

He might well have ended up equalling the idol he replaced.

As it is, we simply have those early years, when a teenage lad from Lancashire stepped into the boots of the greatest player of the age and took the move in his stride, powering Everton back to the pinnacle of the game.

DAVE HICKSON

(243 appearances, 111 goals)

He was the player who would've died for the club; the uncompromising, old-fashioned centre-forward who helped drag Everton out of its Second Division doldrums. He was Dave Hickson, the 'Cannonball Kid'.

Hickson was born in Salford in 1929 but raised in Ellesmere Port. Like most young boys, he fell in love with football, playing games 'behind the wood', alongside the cemetery on Rossmore Road East in Overpool. It was where the boys playing would harbour ambitions of joining the list of greats to come from the town, players like Joe Mercer and Stan Cullis, two Ellesmere Port lads who had gone on to captain the national side.

Hickson, a talented player throughout his youth, was brought to Goodison from non-league Ellesmere Port in May 1948, aged 18. At the time, both Everton and Liverpool had been interested in him but a telling intervention from Hickson's Dad gave the Blues the advantage:

'In my heart I knew where I wanted to go' he later said 'but I was still young and I deferred to my Dad on all the major decisions in my life. Although he was from Salford and had taken me to see United play, like all the best people I think there was a bit of Evertonian in him, and he told me to sign for the Blues'.

Despite his potential, his momentum was halted temporarily by two years of national service. For some, this might have been a set-back, years of vital football development lost. But Hickson was fortunate. While stationed nearby, he began playing for the Cheshire Army Cadets, a side who were coached by none other than Bill 'Dixie' Dean. Like Lawton before him, Hickson ended up learning from the best during his late-teenage years.

According to Hickson, it was thanks to Dean that he became such a strong presence in the air. Although not even Dean could say he shared the same tenacity as his young student. Hickson became defined as a player with an almost reckless sense of courage, often putting his head into places where most would be wary of putting their feet.

Once back at Goodison, with national service completed, the side that Hickson began to slowly break into during the early 1950s was not one of Everton's finest. Back then, the club was ruled by a board which appeared determined to hold on to the austerity aesthetic that had so characterised Britain in the late 1940s: the culture of 'running a tight ship', of 'every penny counts', of 'make do and mend'. In short, they were tight-arses.

As such, the club's prevailing ethos was to put faith in youth (augmented by cheap acquisitions from the lower leagues and Ireland).

It was this approach that led eventually to relegation in 1951. But the misery didn't initially end there. Life in the second tier proved tougher than expected, and, for a time, Everton laboured. At one point, early in the club's second campaign down there, the Blues were bottom of the league – thoughts of an unprecedented drop to the Third Division North haunting those who followed the club.

'It was bleak at times back then' says John Bohanna, who first began going to Goodison in the late-1940s. 'When we first went down hope was thin on the ground. That's part of the reason why a player like Hickson developed such a connection with the fans. He was a ray of light after so much gloom. He gave that sense of hope that had been so sorely absent.'

As the club's second campaign in the second tier had progressed, optimism had slowly grown. The approach of the board might have been largely disastrous, but that isn't to say that the faith in the youth didn't sometimes bear fruit. Young players, such as T. E. Jones, John Willie Parker and Hickson started to make their mark on the first team.

Of these, Hickson was unquestionably the highlight for the fans. Ask any Evertonian who followed the club in the 1950s to name their idol and they will invariably point to the 'Cannonball Kid'.

'He was an old-fashioned centre-forward. With his towering blonde quiff, his physical style and a decent eye for goal, Hickson gave us Blues something to get excited about,' remembers lifelong Evertonian, John Flaherty.

Hickson was tenacious to the point of self-harm. It was a level of commitment appreciated by the Goodison faithful, who responded to a player that appeared to give his heart and soul for the club every Saturday afternoon.

'I think Evertonians, as much as they appreciate skill, have always taken to their hearts players that give everything. And Hickson was the embodiment of that sort of player. That was part of the reason behind the nickname, the "Cannonball Kid". Along with the ferocity of his shot, he was a handful on the pitch, for everyone, including the officials. He put himself about, he argued, he never gave up on anything. Hickson had a strong desire to win the game, and that came out in his personality when he played' Flaherty continues.

If you had to choose one game to illustrate the combative approach of Hickson, to reveal just why Evertonians loved this player so much, it would be the fifth round FA Cup tie that took place against Manchester United on Valentine's Day, 1953.

Everton welcomed the champions to Goodison on the back of an improved spell on the pitch. As 'Stork' reported in the *Liverpool Echo,* a resurgent Everton were not to be underestimated in the cup tie.

'Manchester United will have to sit up and take notice of this Everton team which has not lost a game since January 3. For it has become a competent footballing side with a high degree of confidence in itself.'

Although United went ahead early on, Everton remained in the game and just past the half-hour mark, were rewarded for their efforts when Tommy Eglington equalised, benefitting from wonderful build-up play from Hickson.

The 'Cannonball Kid' had been on great form all afternoon, linking up with Parker and Eglington, winning everything in the air, remaining a constant nuisance to the United defenders. But, five minutes from the break, with the game hammering back and forth, Everton appeared to have been dealt a devastating blow when Hickson dived to connect with a cross, another example of his fearless commitment to the Blue cause. For his efforts, he received a boot to the head. With blood streaming from a cut above his left eye, he was ordered off the field.

'It was typical of Hickson to do something like that'

remembers John Flaherty. 'He was a blood and thunder kind of player. A gladiatorial player. You'd lose count the number of times he did something reckless, going for balls that nobody else would think of going for. He just had that mentality, a desire to win to the point of self-harm.'

Half-time came and went, but without Hickson initially remerging.

Unbeknownst to the crowd, he was being patched up by Harry Cooke, the Everton physio. To the relief of those crammed into Goodison, a few seconds after the Everton side had run out on to the field, that recognisable blonde quiff emerged from the tunnel, complete with a hastily stitched-up wound above his right eye.

Shortly after he returned, as Hickson described in his autobiography, *The Cannonball Kid,* a second collision, this time with the post, almost spelled the end of his game that day:

> 'There was blood and all that everywhere.
> At this point, the referee, Mr. Beacock of
> Scunthorpe, suggested to Peter Farrell [the
> Everton captain] that I should leave the field.
>
> "He'll have to go off," said the referee. "He can't
> go on with an eye like that. He's not normal."

There was no way I was going off the pitch, no way at all. "I am normal," I told him. "Tell him I'm normal, Peter, tell him!" "Of course, you are Dave," said Peter.

"There you are, Ref,' I said. 'I'm staying!"

Blood oozing from his wound, Hickson continued, a decision that ultimately paid off, as the man himself later described:

'On 63 minutes came the game's decisive moment. I took Tommy Eglington's pass on my chest, beat one man, sidestepped another and hammered a right-footed shot beyond the reach of Ray Wood and into the net. Goodison erupted in celebration. It was a wonderful moment.'

The goal was enough to secure the win, giving Evertonians the kind of big Saturday afternoon scalp that had been lacking at Goodison for some time. Although the Blues would get no further than the semi-final, eventually being knocked out by Bolton Wanderers, United's defeat seemed like confirmation that the recent up-turn in form was based on sound foundations, that better things were to come. And in the season that followed, that proved to be the case.

'With Hickson leading the line, and some of the other younger players finding their feet, the side looked better from the beginning. All season we were in the hunt for promotion' remembers John Bo-hanna.

And, according to Bohanna, in contrast to the dirge that had characterised recent campaigns, Everton were also playing attractive, swashbuckling football.

'Along the way, teams were often dispatched by big score-lines. Derby County 6-2, Brentford 6-1, Plymouth 8-4! These were scorelines more in keeping with the Dixie Dean era.'

A key element in this was the partnership that developed between Hickson and Parker. 'He was an excellent inside-forward,' Hickson later wrote of his teammate. 'We had a good working relationship and with that, you always know what the other fellow is doing ... John Willie was really my partner in crime. We each knew what we were going to do.'

There was also, as Hickson explained in *The Cannonball Kid*, an emergent sense of team camaraderie, underlined by a grim determination to reverse the club's fortunes.

'There was a real resolve among us to get Everton back where they belonged in the top-flight. We sat down at the start of the 1953/54 season and resolved to do it. I think the spirit was all over the club.'

As the final game approached, Everton sat outside the promotion positions.

Above them were Leicester City (56 points) and Blackburn Rovers (55). Importantly, both had played their final games, giving Everton (who had 54 points) the opportunity to leapfrog Blackburn and in the process get back into the First Division. And, if the Blues managed the improbable feat of beating Oldham, their next opponents, by a margin of six goals, that would also be enough to see them crowned champions.

'There aren't a lot of Blues left who can remember what it was like to be in the Second Division,' says John Bohanna. 'It was tough. Ever since, whenever we have been down near the bottom of the top-flight, I've had cold sweats and sleepless nights because I know what the reality of relegation is like. We had to get out of that league. It was as simple as that. The last game of the season was as important as any that has taken place in Everton's long history.'

That the club was in any position at all to countenance the idea of promotion was thanks to Hickson's contribution in the season's penultimate game, as the *Liverpool Echo* reported:

'Hickson has scored many extremely valuable goals for Everton but none of greater significance than his splendid header at the 38th minute against Birming-ham. Had it not been for that goal, we should not now be caring two straws about the game at Oldham, as Everton's promotion chances would have been extinguished.'

The game was a late kick-off, so the exodus from Liverpool began early. People took the afternoon off, and by early evening Oldham town centre was awash with Evertonians.

'Oldham had never seen anything like it,' remembers Tony Onslow of the Everton Heritage Society. 'We were there mob-handed. They tried to stop people bunking into the ground by putting tar on the walls. But it made no difference. The young kids just put newspaper over it and climbed over. The tar still got all over them, though. There was a report in the local paper that referred to the young Blues as the "tar ba-bies" of Everton.'

Everton were rampant that day, blowing Oldham off the park. With just 35 minutes gone, they had raced into an unassailable 4-0 lead. Hickson had got him-self the fourth goal, a glorious solo effort that had seen him run half the length of the field, beat three men and drive the ball beyond the keeper's reach.

'It was a goal that sealed promotion in the minds of anyone watching. Everton had been breath-tak-ing and Oldham non-existent. We knew that if we got two more and kept a clean sheet, the title would be ours too. I think at that point most Blues in the ground thought that's exactly what would happen,' says Onslow.

But the title wasn't to be. For all Everton's endeavours, the remaining two goals would not come. Not that it mattered to the Blues who had made the journey.

'Thousands of them swarmed on to the pitch and hoisted Farrell the Everton captain shoulder-high carrying him in triumph to the entrance to the dressing room,' reported Ranger in the *Liverpool Daily Post.*

For Dave Hickson, whose goals and work ethic had done so much to get Everton back into the top-flight, that moment is one that remained with him for his whole life, as he later recalled in *The Cannonball Kid*:

'It was the highlight of my career,' he wrote. 'Even now when people stop me and say, "Hi, Davey", I think it's because they look back at the time when we got them back up to where they are now. I think people remember that time, even if they weren't around to see or experience it. Evertonians are very good with their history and there's a sense of recognition that I was part of a side that got them back to where they belong.'

In the seasons that immediately followed, although

Everton shone in periods, and Parker and Hickson continued to score, under-investment and a lack of quality held the team back. As too did some of the managerial decisions taken by Cliff Britton.

Two games into the 1955/56 season, one such decision had a dramatic impact on the club's relationship with its much-loved centre-forward. Britton dropped Parker and Hickson, and in response, the 'Cannonball Kid', asked for a transfer. It was the tipping point for Hickson, the last straw. He was frustrated by a board and a manager who he felt were stopping the club from reaching its potential. Within a fortnight he was at Aston Villa, sold for £19,500.

It turned out to be an unhappy move. Hickson failed to settle in the Midlands and so found himself on the road again after just two months, ending up at Huddersfield Town – this time for a fee of £16,000. Although he performed well at Leeds Road, he'd joined a side in decline and could only watch on as the Yorkshiremen slipped into the Second Division at the season's end.

But to the delight of Evertonians, the Dave Hickson story at the club wasn't over yet. After averaging better than a goal every two games for Huddersfield, Hickson delighted Blues by returning to Goodison in the summer of 1957, in a move he described at the time as 'one of the happiest moments in my life'.

'It was great to have him back' says John Flaherty. 'Hickson was always a crowd favourite and he'd been missed by the fans. To see him coming out and playing for us again, was just what we wanted.'

Though Everton languished in the wrong half of the table, Hickson continued to hit the target regularly, remaining great value for the modest outlay. But when a new manager arrived at Goodison, Johnny Carey replacing the outgoing Ian Buchan in 1958, a change was in the air. Carey was in the mood for re-jigging the struggling squad and as part of that signed off on a controversial move, selling the 30-year-old Hickson to Liverpool for £12,500.

The shock move created outrage at the time. So incensed were some Evertonians, and so committed to their idol, that they claimed they were willing to defect to Anfield. While there were those amongst the red half of the city who vowed that they would give up supporting their beloved club in protest, furious at the arrival of a player who was so indelibly connected to Goodison.

In the end, Hickson proved to be a hit, silencing the naysayers with his committed performances. His cause was inevitably helped by the fact that on his Liverpool debut, at home to Aston Villa, he scored both goals in a 2-1 victory – one of them a trademark diving header.

Despite thriving across the Park, the arrival of Ian St John in May 1961 would ultimately spell the end for Hickson's Anfield dalliance, and in the summer of that same year, he was released to join non-league Cambridge City.

But he was not finished with the Football League just yet. After a fleeting sojourn at Cambridge, he returned briefly with Second Division Bury early in 1962. From there, he then completed a full-house of Merseyside employers by spending two seasons with Tranmere Rovers, then playing in the fourth tier.

The move to Prenton Park gave him the rare honour of being one of only a handful of players to have turned out for three Merseyside clubs, joining John Heydon and Frank Mitchell, who also played for Everton, Liverpool and Tranmere Rovers, and Bill Lacey and Neil McBain, both of whom played for Everton, Liverpool and New Brighton.

Hickson scored regularly at Tranmere, before finishing off his career by taking several player-manager positions at clubs including Ballymena United, Bangor and Elsmere Port.

But despite his many moves, his heart always belonged to Everton. 'I've been to a few clubs, great clubs' he once said, 'Aston Villa, Huddersfield, Liverpool. But Everton... there's something magic about it. I'm just an Evertonian that's all.'

It was a love that was repaid by Bill Kenwright when he asked Hickson if he wanted to 'come back home' to Goodison after he retired, working there as a match-day host and stadium tour guide, giving generations of Evertonians the chance to spend time with the great man.

He passed away in July 2013, aged 83, after giving decades of service to the Blues. Along with the goals he scored, Hickson left behind a footballing legacy to be proud of and possibly one of the greatest ever quotes to encapsulate a player's love for their club:

'I would have died for Everton; he said 'I would have broken every other bone in my body for any other club I played for but I would have died for this club.'

ALEX YOUNG

(275 appearances, 89 goals)

'Without any doubt the finest "true" footballer it has ever been my privilege to worship. And those who were lucky enough to have seen Alex play did worship him. Our own "Golden Vision". A title accepted immediately': Bill Kenwright.

Alex Young is the player who doesn't fit the mould. In the long history of the titans who have worn the 'Number 9' shirt, he is the outlier, the aberration. He sits uneasily amongst the panoply of Goodison greats, a forward who was not big or strong.

'Alex Young was slight, nimble and delicate; someone who had the build of a winger or inside-forward,' recalls George McKane of the Everton Supporters Trust. 'He was a one-off, a supremely gifted player, the likes that you rarely see. He had a beautiful touch and could ghost past big lumbering centre-halves with ease [the kind with hairy arms and Desperate Dan chins] and had the knack to be in the right place at the right time. When you watched him in action, it was an honour.'

Young was born in 1937, in Loanhead, a mining village in Midlothian. Like many of his age and class from that area, a life at the coalface seemed to beckon and aged 15 he was taken on as an apprentice at Burghlee colliery. But for Young, his life at the mine would be short-lived. Spotted by Hearts while playing youth football, this boyhood Hibs fan was taken on by the club.

There he spent a few years dividing his time between the Burghlee colliery and Tynecastle, a foot in both worlds. But increasingly, it was his skill with a ball that dictated the path his life would take. His debut for Hearts came, aged 18, in a League Cup tie at the beginning of the 1955/56 season. Despite his tender years, it didn't take long for the fans and his manager to appreciate the young forward's talents. By the campaign's end, he was already a regular in the side and a favourite on the terraces. In five years with Hearts, Young found the net 71 times in 155 appearances, helping Tommy Walker's side to an array of silverware, including two league titles.

With a growing reputation as a forward possessed of rare skill and grace, as well as potency in front of goal, Young began to attract admirers. First, the national side came calling and in May 1960, he won his debut cap against Austria (there would be ten more). And next, teams from England began sniffing around.

Although initially loath to move, Young's journey south was ultimately precipitated via a falling out with Walker. After being singled out for criticism following a languid performance against Dundee United, Young broke the habit of a lifetime and verbally retaliated. It was the beginning of the end.

When the suitors came, Everton and Preston North

End led the pack, with the latter in pole position. Hearts accepted Preston's bid and Young agreed personal terms. But the move never went through, as the man himself revealed in an interview with the Everton forum, *NSNO* back in 2008: 'I went to Preston and they said that they were going to give me £3000. That was a lot of money then, you could buy a house with that; plenty of money. I said "well if you do that then I will come to you"; that was the first meeting. The next day, the Preston manager came again and said "the directors won't give you £3000, it's £2000", so I said "Everton's giving me £2000, I'll go to Everton".' And with that, in November 1960, Everton signed a Goodison legend and Preston missed out on a centre-forward who could have transformed their fortunes.

Although injuries marred his first season with the Blues, flashes of what Young could do were noted by those watching. 'Young is a thoroughbred, a great mover with the ball, fast, active, razor-sharp in his reactions' reported the *Liverpool Echo* after one impressive performance.

He soon got over his fitness issues and for the next three seasons was unassailable; his form breath-taking. 'He formed a great partnership with Roy Vernon, who always has to be remembered for the work he did with Young, and the pair of them helped us reach heights that hadn't been seen at Goodison for some time,' remembers George McKane.

The pair netted 116 league goals between them over three seasons, lifting the club to the higher reaches of the table and helping Everton clinch the title in 1963, their first piece of post-war silverware and first title win in a generation. There was one goal scored by Young during the run-in that for those who followed the club at the time, will always stand out:

'There was just a few games left and we were vying for the championship with Leicester and Spurs. We had Spurs at home in one of those games where you knew that if we won, it would give us an edge,' remembers Dr David France, the man behind the Everton Collection.

67,500 people crammed into Goodison to watch that game, eager to see the Blues land a telling blow against their title rivals. Although a more open game than when they had last met, a tight 0-0 at White Hart Lane earlier in the season, there would only be one goal to separate the sides, and it arrived 20 minutes in, to the delight of the Evertonians.

'I remember Roy Vernon, out on the wing, putting a cross into the box', recalls France. 'There, Alex rose to meet it majestically, leaping above John Smith, the statuesque Spurs-centre half, who must have had a few inches on him. I remember his head turned through 90 degrees, eyes on the ball as it sailed past the keeper and into the net. It was a thing of beauty.'

While in his pomp during the first half of the 1960s, Young was simply sublime. As Michael Durkin reminisced on *ToffeeWeb*, to watch him was to be in the presence of something majestic, almost spiritual. He first saw Young on a wintry afternoon against Leeds, the nimble forward marked by two snarling defenders:

'I can still see him in that game with two young Leeds players facing him. One of them was an aggressive young South African player named Gerry Francis. Alex killed the glistening orange ball to feet in a flurry of snow crystals and Francis snarled to his team-mate, 'Gerrim'!!! Except the tackle arrived in empty space. Alex was gone. For a microsecond, the defenders looked at each other. Over the years, I got used to that look on opponents' faces. It was an almost comical combination of bafflement, fury and hapless despair. Seeing Alex play for the first time was like an epiphany. You wanted to shout 'Hallelujah!'

Young's God-like status amongst Evertonians was only enhanced by the moniker for which he would always be known, 'The Golden Vision'. But although adopted by Evertonians, the name did not originate from within Goodison. Instead, it was coined by Danny Blanchflower, captain of both Northern Ireland and Bill Nicholson's great Spurs sides of the early 1960s. In Young he believed there was something beyond football: 'The view every Saturday that we have of a more perfect world, a world that has got a pattern and is finite,' said Blanchflower. 'And that's Alex, The Golden Vision.'

Despite his talents, Young endured a troubled relationship with Harry Catterick the manager who had brought him to Goodison. In no small part, this was attributable to the adulation given to him by the crowd. As Young later recalled: 'It turned out that the more the fans loved me, the more the manager disliked me. I was engaged in a constant battle with Harry and learned not to trust him.'

It probably didn't help matters that during one league game, in the 1966 season, a fan ran onto the pitch holding aloft a banner that read 'Sack Catterick, Keep Young' in response to their idol being dropped in favour of the teenage Joe Royle.

Dropped, often played out of position and with rumours that Catterick was keen to cash in on his asset on more than one occasion, it appeared that Young was right to be wary. According to Rob Sawyer, author of *Harry Catterick: The Untold Story of a Football Great*, the Everton manager was a dour and foreboding figure, somebody unlikely to look kindly on a player being so obviously loved by the crowd. 'He was a product of his times, a man who had grown up in the more austere environment of the 1920s and

1930s; very old school. He believed that the manager was the most important figure at the club. The players were there to do his bidding. If there was a hierarchy, he was at the top.'

Beyond the snippets available on YouTube, for those who wish to reminisce about Young's glory, or those who simply want to watch the legend in action, there is an idiosyncratic remnant of 1960s working-class drama that can sate that particular hunger. Long before *Looking for Eric*, there was *The Golden Vision*, Ken Loach's docu-drama, made for the BBC as a Wednesday Play, which focused on the historic bond between a football club and its fans. The film switches between interviews with Everton players and dramatised scenes from the lives of fans, played by local actors like Bill Dean, Neville Smith and Ken Jones.

Young, as the title suggests, is the centre of the film from the playing side. And the contrast between him and the fictitious fans is a stark one. Where their lives, centred around football, family and work, appear certain, albeit simultaneously chaotic, Young's seems to be one characterised by self-awareness, doubt and uncertainty. As a slice of working-class life, it's as good as anything Loach has ever made. And as an exploration of the role that football played, and arguably continues to play, in such communities, it's up there with the best.

But, for an Evertonian, what's more appealing is the capturing of one of the club's idols as he really was. It's easy to forget, when players are lionised and pass into immortality, that they are just people. Young's normalcy and decency, just a working-class lad trying his best, comes across. You see the man, not The Golden Vision, (despite the play's title).

Ironically, by the time The Golden Vision was made, Young's relationship with Everton was drawing to a close. The Blues were changing and the side that had been so synonymous with Young, the first that Catterick had built at Goodison, was on its way to being replaced by the one that would come to be defined by the 'Holy Trinity' of Harvey, Kendall and Ball, and which would go on to claim the title in 1970.

But, even as his relevance at Goodison started to ebb, for a time Young still remained a player who could thrill. At the close of the 1966/67 season, Everton hosted Sunderland at home. The Blues, still in transition, were on course to finish sixth. Sunderland, not long out of the second tier, were in the bottom eight but safe. There was little but pride riding on the game. Few expected much. But what they got was a pleasant surprise; an Alex Young masterclass.

'Young beat Sunderland almost on his own that night' the Everton captain, Brian Labone, wrote in his autobiography, *Defence at the Top.*

From the first whistle, The Golden Vision delighted the crowd. He zipped, danced and buzzed around the pitch, linking with his team-mates, creating chances for others and accepting some for himself, as Everton dominated the visitors. Unsurprisingly, considering that he was at the heart of everything good Everton produced, Young played a part in the opener when he slid a delightful pass to Johnny Morrissey to put him one-on-one with the keeper, and Everton went 1-0 up as half-time approached.

In the second period, Everton's dominance continued and inevitably more goals arrived. The second came not long after the restart, when Young and Jimmy Husband combined well to get the ball wide to Alan Ball. His low centre was met spectacularly by Morrissey, who volleyed Everton into a 2-0 lead. Minutes later, Colin Harvey made it 3-0, converting Husband's cross (he had been threaded through by Young) to put the game beyond Sunderland.

Although the visitors pulled one back late on, it was a rare foray forward against a tsunami of Everton attacks. As the game ebbed to a close, Everton won a penalty which was converted by Morrissey. But although he had completed his hat-trick, the players wanted the match-ball to go to Young, so peerless had his performance been; a dazzling display of grace, vision and skill.

Frustratingly for his legions of fans, such afternoons became a thing of the past from then on. After that season, Young's strike rate declined and his powers appeared to wane more dramatically. Although still loved, the hints of decline that had only fleetingly been felt before became more pronounced.

In May 1968, after eight years in which he had delighted the fans, the curtain came down on one of Goodison's most cherished careers. With it evident that the club was no longer interested in his services, Young set up a potentially lucrative move to the short-lived New York Generals franchise. But once again the troubled relationship with Catterick came to impact his career. The Everton manager blocked the move and so Young found himself looking for something closer to home.

In the end, he left to become player/manager with Northern Irish club Glentoran, fulfilling a long-held desire to move into coaching. Sadly, the move was brief, Young's failing hearing forcing him to step down early in his tenure. Following that stint in Northern Ireland, he then moved on to Stockport County where after 23 games a knee injury eventually forced his retirement aged 32.

After leaving football, Young returned to Scotland, where he lived a quiet, largely anonymous post-football existence, first running a pub, then after a spell of unemployment, buying into the Edinburgh-based upholstery firm of Richard Wylie Ltd.

If he ever tired of the anonymity, there were always reminders of his former glory on occasional trips back to Goodison, as his wife, Nancy reminisced to *NSNO* shortly before his death in 2017:

'Whenever we go back to Liverpool people always recognise Alex. Hardly anybody in Scotland does or if they do, they don't let on. His status among Evertonians never fails to surprise me. It's been an awful long time now but people still adore him.'

Adoration is a rare thing at Goodison. Unlike the neighbours across Park, it is not given away easily. It has to be earned. More often than not, it's achieved through grit and determination, by players who seem willing to die for the shirt. But occasionally, as with Young, talent alone is enough.

'Alex Young is probably the most gifted player to ever pull on the blue shirt,' argues John Bohanna. 'And it's a testament to his talent that his name continues to be known amongst Evertonians today. He will never be forgotten. Our Alex, Golden, Visionary.'

JOE ROYLE

(276 appearances, 119 goals)

As first games went, it was something of a baptism of fire. The young Joe Royle, then just 16, had been called into Harry Catterick's office the afternoon before, believing he was going there for a dressing down from the notorious disciplinarian. But to his surprise, Royle found out that he would be in the starting eleven the next day, to face Blackpool at Bloomfield Road.

As if this wasn't surprising enough for a young player, it would turn out that Royle would be deputising for crowd favourite, Alex Young, who Catterick had controversially decided to drop. Prior to his decision, Catterick had noticed signs of complacency in Young's play. With an FA Cup third-round tie with Sunderland the following week being Everton's only remaining route to silverware, he decided to provide the listless Young with a sharp reminder that nobody was an automatic pick, hoping that the shock might jolt the Scot's season back into action.

Any debut so young would have been a test of character. But to do it in those circumstances must've added an extra weight on Royle's shoulders. And perhaps it was this that led to his less-than-impressive showing. The gangly teenager who led the Everton line that afternoon struggled, joining the rest of the team in a laboured 2-0 defeat to the Seasiders.

After the game, the travelling Blues were in uproar, with some opting to stay behind to protest at Young's omission. Eventually, the players came out to be greeted by their complaints, which increased in volume when Catterick appeared. As the manager was about to get on the coach, there was a surge forward and he was pushed to the ground in the melee.

It was an extraordinary response, one that revealed the size of the shoes that Royle would be tasked with one day filling. And yet, he remained undaunted. Royle was a true Evertonian, and the prospect of playing regularly for his boyhood club was irresistible.

His relationship with Everton had started when he was a small child. 'I'd been going to watch the Blues since I was seven or eight' Royle says. 'I used to go in the paddock. If you look at the ground now from the Main Stand, there's still a wooden panel where the clock used to be. That's where I stood.'

As a youngster, several clubs were interested in signing Royle, including Manchester United. But it was his hometown club that succeeded in recruiting him to their ranks, Everton taking him on as an apprentice in 1964.

'Everton were my team, although my father was a Manc. I remember him being quite thrilled about Manchester United being interested in me. But I wanted to join Everton. I had a lot of clubs interested but they were always my first choice. And, importantly, they moved quicker than anyone else in getting me to sign.'

Although he made a smattering of appearances in the season that followed his debut, it was during the 1967/68 campaign that Royle first began to feature more regularly.

'When Joe first broke into the team I wasn't overly impressed' admits lifelong Blue, Brian Roach. 'The fact that it probably spelled the end of Alex Young most likely played a part in that. But, like most fans, a few goals changed things. Early on, he and Alex played in the same team, Joe at centre forward and Alex on the right side of midfield. That didn't last long, Joe was improving all the time and getting the goals.'

The 20 goals he scored in 40 starts during the 1967/68 season suggested that Catterick had been right to put faith in the youngster. As Young moved on to pastures new at the end of campaign, it looked as though the side already had a ready-made replacement. But it was one who also helped create a different kind of Everton:

'Joe changed the team dynamic' says Roach. 'Alex Young liked the ball to his feet, but Joe was more of a target man, and a very good one, he would win a lot of ball. He used to jump early, that was his trick. He'd be in the air and the centre half couldn't see the ball, this meant he was on the way down when he headed it.'

But, as Roach explains, there was more to Royle's game than simply operating as a battering ram:

'He had a great first touch and he passed the ball well too. There was a creative side to him. And for a striker he was unselfish in that he would always pass to a better-placed teammate. And he was an excellent finisher, powerful right foot and nerves of steel.'

Once established in the first team, Royle would become the focal point of one of the great Everton sides of the previous century.

As the 1960s came to a close, a process of transition at Goodison that had begun under Catterick a few years earlier, one that saw him try to move on from his 1963 title-winning side, was starting to bear fruit. Slowly, a team emerged that not only looked like it had what it took to match the achievements of 1963, but one that also looked capable of reaching even greater heights.

'It was a side that bristled with talent,' remembers the former Everton defender Roger Kenyon. 'Along with the players who had been there for a while, like Gordon West in goal and Brian Labone at the back, Catterick brought in some great new players, such as Alan Ball and Howard Kendall, and promoted youngsters from the club, including Colin Harvey, Joe Royle and Alan Whittle. It took a while to take shape, but when it started to, you felt there was something special there.'

During the latter half of the 1967/68 season, the first signs that Catterick was on to something good began to emerge. Everton reached the final of the FA Cup (dominating West Brom but unfortunately losing) and, in the league, finished fifth, just six points behind winners Manchester City.

'Everton had always been a good footballing side under Harry,' remembers Royle, 'but around that time, something started to click. We were playing some wonderful football and that only got better in the season that followed.'

In terms of aesthetic beauty, the 1968/69 season is regarded by many as one of the finest ever seen at Goodison.

'They were a wonderful footballing side,' recalls John Daley, who first began going to Goodison in the 1950s, 'one that played without inhibition and which were a joy to watch. But also, perhaps because they lacked maturity, one that couldn't always grind out a result or make dominance count.'

Despite this, as the 1968/69 run-in approached,

Everton were just about in with a shout at the title. But a few injury issues, a fixture pile-up and that touch of inexperience, conspired to halt any assault at the top. Everton drew too many of those remaining matches and ended up third, ten points behind winners Leeds United.

'Even though the end of the season was slightly frustrating,' says Royle, 'there were still plenty of positives. We had knitted together well as a side and were playing some wonderful football. And personally, I was on great form. I scored 29 that season, wearing the iconic "Number 9" shirt. It was the best total I ever scored for the club in one campaign. All in, we felt like the side was gelling and as the following season started, we thought we'd be strong contenders.'

And they were. Playing a notional 4–3–3 formation from the off (which could convert to a 4–4–2 in defence), Everton were sensational all year: fast, organised and strong.

'People have used the phrase, in relation to Everton, of "instant football",' said Catterick in an interview with ITV around that time. 'I think', he continued, 'it is a compliment because we believe in quick play, quick, accurate passing and possession until we can see an opening and then striking as quickly as possible. Instant football means, in effect, that you have got quick control and the ability to part with the ball quickly and accurately.'

Although there were dips and times when the fans might have thought that another near miss was on the cards, Everton remained in the hunt and as the run-in approached appeared to be favourites to claim the top prize.

'There was a 2–0 victory against Liverpool in March at their place,' recalls Royle, 'with goals from Alan Whittle and me, when I think we all thought that the title would be ours. We were playing so well and winning important games. As good as our rivals were, I think we knew that we were something special by then.'

With two games to spare the title was eventually clinched at Goodison with a 2-0 win against West Brom at the beginning of April. 'The atmosphere that day was incredible,' remembers John Daley. 'There were chants of "Ever-ton", "We are the champions" and "We're on our way to Europe" ringing out. You must have been able to hear it from miles away.'

After the final whistle, the players did a lap of honour, soaking up the adulation from the thousands who had crammed themselves into Goodison.

'The sense of elation was palpable,' remembers Royle. 'And we felt it was just the start of something. We had a young team, a great manager and we all felt that this side could go on to dominate. That things could only get better.'

And yet, as is so often the case with Everton, that sense of future promise ended up proving to be illusory.

'There was a slight hangover from the 1970 World Cup which didn't help the side's title defence but more than that, Everton and Catterick just seemed to lose momentum. It didn't help that players left the club, most notably Alan Ball. The Holy Trinity just wasn't the same with one of its key members gone. But equally, I think Catterick just couldn't conjure up the magic again. He'd already rebuilt once and maybe after a decade at the club, he'd run out of ideas. Certainly, by the time that ill-health forced him to step down in 1973 there was already a sense that his best days were behind him' says John Flaherty.

For Royle, looking back on those days, there was a moment when he felt the hope that had been evident when that title was lifted had dissipated.

'There was a week in late March 1971 when that great Catterick side died' he says. 'Our title defence by that point was well and truly over. But we had the European Cup and the FA Cup still in our sights. In the former, we faced Panathinaikos in the quarter-finals and in the latter we had Liverpool in the semis.'

The Greeks were battered at Goodison but somehow managed to earn a 1–1 draw (nicking a vital away goal). This meant the Blues would need to take the game to Panathinaikos in the away leg to continue on their European adventure.

On a terrible, dusty playing surface, in front of an exceptionally hostile crowd (one that drenched the Everton bench in spit) and ruled over by a referee whose impartiality has long been questioned, the Blues stumbled, the game ending goalless, meaning they were knocked out on the away-goals rule.

A season that had promised so much was effectively ended a few days later when, exhausted after their Greek Odyssey, Everton were knocked out of the FA Cup by Liverpool.

'You can never know what would have happened had we got through against Panathinaikos or Liverpool,' says Royle. 'Either could have been the spark that brought things back to life. But in the end, those two results killed the side off. And it's a pity because the talent was there to do remarkable things, as we proved against Borussia Mönchengladbach earlier in the European Cup. Knocking them out was no small achievement. But it counted for nothing in the end. We just didn't have the luck or the momentum to keep going.'

For Royle, injuries would plague much of his remaining time with the Blues, taking the throttle off his Everton career. By the mid-1970s, the arrival of a new manager in Billy Bingham, the signing of new players, such as Bob Latchford, and Royle's continued struggles with fitness and form meant that a move away from Goodison seemed inevitable.

'It was a hard time and the thought of leaving Everton was difficult. But in the end, it happened. An offer came in from Manchester City and I found myself off to Maine Road.'

The £170,000 arrival initially struggled, scoring just once in 16 League games, after moving there towards the end of December 1974. But in his second season at the club, injury-free, the old Royle magic returned. In 1975/76, only Dennis Tueart's 24 goals beat his overall total of 18. What's more, he crowned his first full season with City by playing on the winning side as Newcastle were beaten in the League Cup Final.

In late 1977, Royle left Maine Road, moving to Bristol City for a few seasons and then to Norwich City, where he would see out his playing days, eventually retiring due to a knee injury in 1982.

'Ironically, my last game as a player was at Goodison. I scored and Norwich won but I still got a standing ovation. As I came off, the Norwich manager at the time, Ken Brown, said he'd never heard anything like it before' remembers Royle.

But, of course, his connection with Everton did not end with retirement from the game. Despite leaving the club in the mid-1970s, he always remained an Evertonian. Years later, when the club was staring into the abyss and looking for a saviour, it was Royle who answered the call.

After retirement from the playing side, he had immediately taken over the managerial reins at Oldham Athletic, spending twelve years in charge at Boundary Park. During that time, he took the club into the First Division in 1991 and managed to reach the 1990 League Cup final (losing to Nottingham Forest) and the last four of the FA Cup twice (in 1990 and 1994), losing both times to Manchester United in a replay.

In the autumn of 1994, Everton were bottom of the league and manager-less, following the sacking of the hapless Mike Walker. The Blues were desperate and in dire need of someone to haul them out of the mire. Royle took up the challenge, starting his resurrection project with a hard-fought home win over Liverpool.

'That win was momentous' says Stan Osborne author of *Making the Grade,* his memories of being a youth player at the club during the late-1960s and early-1970s. 'The confidence it gave, combined with the combative set-up Royle put in place, set us on the road to recovery. I think the form after that point would have put us in the top eight that's how dramatic the turnaround was. And it had to be. Despite all his efforts, Everton only secured safety with one game to spare. It was a herculean effort, one that illustrated just what a great manager Royle was at Everton.'

And, as the icing on the cake, that season was capped off with an improbable FA Cup win. Despite fighting for their lives for months, the Blues managed to go all the way in the cup, beating Manchester United 1-0 in the final.

'The 1990s were a fairly bleak time to be an Evertonian' says Simon Hart, author of *Here We Go: Everton in the 1980s*. 'But Royle added a bit of light to all that darkness. Not only did he save our skin, but he also gave the club its last piece of silverware. When you add that to what he achieved when he was a player with us, you can appreciate why he's sometimes referred to as "Mr Everton". He's done so much for our club, a true Everton great.'

BOB LATCHFORD

(289 appearances, 138 goals)

Amongst the cavalcade of forwards taken to the hearts of Evertonians, Bob Latchford has a special place.

'At a time when we looked enviously across Stanley Park at the success that we had once thought was ours to take, a time when people would go into school and work and endure the daily smugness of Liverpudlians, a time when you felt so much in Liverpool's shadow, Bob Latchford was something magical, a class player that Liverpool didn't have. And that mattered' says Brian Viner, author of *Looking for the Toffees: In Search of the Heroes of Everton*.

Latchford was born in Birmingham in 1951, into a family in which football was in the blood. His elder brother, David became a goalkeeper at Birmingham City, while a younger brother, Peter, another goalkeeper, played for West Brom and Celtic.

But for Latchford, it was always about scoring not saving goals. After impressing at junior level, he joined his brother at Birmingham, making his debut in March 1969, the 18-year-old scoring twice in a 3-1 win over Preston North End.

Despite that impressive start to life at St Andrews, he only made four further appearances that season and managed only ten more in the following campaign. But he prodded and pushed, slowly making himself a contender at Birmingham. By the end of the 1970-71 season, he had become a regular in the side, primed to launch himself at Division Two.

There, in the 1971-72 campaign, the football world first began to realise what he was capable of. His 23 League goals helped the club secure promotion to the top-flight for the first time in 32 years.

A continued eye for goal in the club's first season up, caught the attention of a few top-flight managers, including Everton's boss at the time, Billy Bingham. With cash in the bank and in desperate need of a for-ward, Bingham came in with a bid. But Birmingham City (who were struggling to avoid relegation) were adamant that no amount of money could take him away.

After plenty of back and forth, a compromise be-tween Bingham and the Birmingham manager, Fred-die Goodwin, was eventually secured. Birmingham would allow Latchford to leave if they could get a top-class midfielder and a defender in return. What this meant was Howard Kendall and Archie Styles, plus £80,000 in a deal worth £350,000 - a British record fee at the time.

The deal had left Bingham with a tough choice to make. The need for a new striker at Everton was palpable. In the past two campaigns, the Blues had managed the meagre return of less than a goal a game. By the time the deal had been struck in February 1974, the return was only fractionally above that. But as much as Everton needed a forward, the sacrifice required was no small one. Although Styles was only a fringe presence, and not a promising one at that, Kendall had been Everton's best player in recent years. Aged 28, he was still in his prime and as a one-time member of the beloved 'Holy Trinity', remained a crowd favourite.

Ultimately, Bingham had gone for goals. But, however understandable, the move did not go down well amongst the fans, causing outrage amongst Blues. The letters pages of the *Liverpool Echo* were inundated with complaints, illustrating how highly Kendall was still regarded amongst Evertonians.

It placed an extra level of expectation on the head of the new arrival, who was already feeling the pressure of that transfer fee, as he explained to *The Football Pink* in 2015:

'I carried the burden until I got my first goal for the club. I didn't score in my first two games for Everton, but then I opened my account against Leicester City and the great weight was lifted.'

And once he got going, Latchford kept at it. In his first full season, he scored 17 league goals as Everton finished fourth, just three points behind champions Derby County, having led the First Division into

April.

'We should have won the title,' he later said 'We had two really bad results against Carlisle, who finished bottom. We were 2-0 up at Goodison and lost 3-2 and they turned us over 3-0 away. If we'd beaten them twice, we'd have won the League by a point. That's how close we came.'

First, under Bingham and then under his successor, Gordon Lee, Latchford constantly provided the kind of firepower that could lift a side, giving it the realistic prospect of challenging for silverware.

'He was great to watch,' remembers Viner. 'He didn't score great goals, like bending free kicks or thirty-yard screamers. But he was big, strong and powerful and read the game superbly. He seemed to always be in the right place at the right time – a natural born goal scorer.'

But, although they came close on several occasions, challenging for the title a few times and losing the League Cup final in 1977, his life with Everton would never be marked by top-level success.

'We qualified for Europe, we got to FA Cup semi-finals, we were competing for championships,' he later said. 'But it was dark days because we ended up coming short. And Liverpool were so dominant, which made it harder.'

And so, he had to make do with a different kind of glory, an achievement for which Evertonians, and those outside the club, still know him best for: the 30-goal season.

Ahead of the 1977/78 campaign, the *Daily Express* had offered a £10,000 prize (no small amount by the standards of the time) to the first player that scored 30 league goals in the First Division that season. Latchford, despite topping the Everton scoring charts three years in a row and bagging 17 league goals in the previous campaign, was not considered a favourite by the bookies.

'I think us Blues gave him a better shot though. We were playing good football and he seemed as decent a bet as anyone to reach that target first,' remembers Dave Prentice, lifelong Blue and the *Liverpool Echo's* head of sport.

Although his failure to get on the scoresheet in the first three games of the season might have dented any initial confidence, Latchford did eventually start to pick up goals.

'He would go a few games without scoring and then bang in four against QPR or three against Coventry. So, just when you thought he might not do it, he'd suddenly and dramatically remind you just what he was capable of' continues Prentice.

Along with Everton's more attack-minded football that season, which inevitably gave the club's forwards more opportunities, Latchford also benefitted from the arrival in the summer of Dave Thomas from QPR.

'Thomas was a fantastic winger and he could put a cross into the box on a sixpence,' remembers Brian Viner. 'He was the perfect supplier for a forward like Latchford, someone who was so predatory in front of goal. The two of them seemed to understand each other, know exactly what the other had in mind. It was one of Gordon Lee's better moves.'

Despite Latchford's potency and Everton's sparkling form, the 1977/78 season ended up being a frustrating one for Evertonians. A hoped-for title challenge had ultimately stuttered. As the run-in approached, the Blues had fallen off the pace. Although European football was secured, the fans were left with the lingering sense that the side could have done more.

To make matters worse, Liverpool had once again reached the final of the European Cup, where they had the opportunity to defend their title against the unfancied Club Brugge.

'The sole silver lining for us Blues was Latchford,' says Viner. 'As the season had closed, he'd got closer and closer to the magic number. By the end, at a home game against Chelsea, he needed two goals to get himself over the finishing line. For Evertonians back then, him doing that would be our "title", our "European Cup". It was that important.'

On the day itself, Latchford recalls feeling pretty relaxed. 'I was very calm all day,' he recently told *Toffee TV.* 'I woke up very calm, which is unusual as I always had a little bit of tension ... but on that day, nothing. Just a total calm. I knew I was going to get the two goals.'

Although he might have been strangely relaxed, for those in the ground, it was a different story:

'There was a palpable sense of tension in the air,' recalls Dave Prentice. 'You could feel it. 40,000 nervous fans crowded into Goodison on that Saturday afternoon to see if Everton's number nine could reach that magical target.'

Everton made mincemeat of the Londoners that day, dominating them throughout. 'We strolled to 2–0 lead within 15 minutes,' continues Prentice, 'and it could have been more. Chelsea were overwhelmed and Everton were magnificent. But the strange thing was, I don't think anyone really cared about winning or losing. They had come to see Latchford score and so when Dobson and Wright got the opening goals, the crowd wasn't that bothered.'

The scoreline remained the same until the 54th minute, when Neal Robinson, the 21-year-old rookie right-back, scored his first (and what would prove to be only) goal for the club.

'You have to feel for him,' says Brian Viner. 'What should have been a glorious moment for the youngster was marred slightly by the muted reaction. By that point we were all starting to get a bit impatient and were even less interested in other players scoring than we had been at the start of the match!'

Although Everton were rampant, and Chelsea largely passive, as the minutes ticked along it looked to those watching as though Latchford might fall at the final hurdle.

'We were just beginning to think it wasn't to be,' remembers Viner, 'when Mick Buckley put a cross into the box and Latchford was able to get on the end of it to get his 29th. The noise from the crowd was incredible. You'd have thought it was a cup final or something.'

Mick Lyons added a fifth not long after, leaping in front of Latchford to head home from a corner. Everton's stalwart centre-half then further tested the patience of Everton's centre-forward when he got up top again, latched on to a loose ball and thundered a shot against the crossbar.

In a recent interview with the writer and Evertonian, Andreas Selliaas, Latchford revealed that his response to Lyons's effort suggested that the pressure was finally getting to him:

'Mick Lyons is the toughest player ever to play for Everton and I've never had a negative word to say against him, before or now. But the pressure was immense that day to get to 30, and when Mick hit the crossbar instead of passing, I shouted at him "Fuck off, Lyonsy, and stay in our half!"'

Luckily for Latchford, it was advice that his captain opted to ignore. Not long after, the Chelsea centre-half, Micky Droy challenged Lyons in the box, and the Everton captain went to ground. In all honesty, it was a bit of a soft penalty, but it didn't matter. The referee signalled to the spot and Goodison roared its approval.

Remarkably, nearly all of the goals Latchford had scored to that point had come from open play. Penalties were not usually his responsibility. But this opportunity wouldn't be passed. There was only one man to take that spot-kick. He duly stepped up to grasp his date with destiny.

Latchford took up the story in his autobiography, *A Different Road*: 'Martin Dobson took me to one side while Chelsea began to protest. "Just keep your head down and blast it," he whispered. I followed his advice. I thought about exactly where I wanted to put the ball – to Bonetti's right-hand side. There were no nerves. The excitement cancelled out my fear and I was feeling numb. I was simply waiting for the whistle. This was my big chance. The ball left my right foot, I closed my eyes and then heard the Goodison roar. Elation. Relief. Satisfaction. I ran to the supporters and sunk to my knees. As fans ran on to the pitch, my team-mates ran towards me. The fairy tale was complete.'

It was not the greatest penalty that you'll ever see, but it did the job. Everton were 6–0 up and Latchford had got his 30.

'I think up to that point, that was my greatest moment as a Blue,' says Brian Viner. 'I had never experienced an atmosphere like it. The whole place was rocking. You have to appreciate how important that goal was. In a decade when so little had gone right for Everton, that was a moment to truly cherish. Bobby Latchford walked on water. And he was ours!'

In theory, that goal should have made Latchford better off. But true to his self-effacing, modest style, he gave half the prize money to the PFA and £4,000 to his teammates, keeping just £1,000 for himself.

'The money side of the award is secondary to me' he later said 'The prestige and sense of achievement in reaching the record is the part that has thrilled me.'

Latchford would remain at Everton for a further few seasons; a key part of Gordon Lee's attempts to resurrect the club's fortunes. As with Bingham before him, despite moments of promise, and Latchford's goals, Lee was never able to succeed and lost his job in May 1981. He was replaced by Howard Kendall, who joined from Blackburn Rovers where he had been turning heads as player/manager.

In a reverse of what had happened when Latchford had arrived at Goodison, Kendall's return acted as a prelude to his own exit, sold to Swansea City for £125,000. Not that the new manager wanted him to leave, as Latchford revealed to *The Football Pink*:

'It was my decision. I just felt that the club had started going backwards and I started to have doubts. I also had probably my worst injury in 1980-81. I damaged my hamstring in the November and then I didn't play again until the final league game of the season and I think that, coupled with the fact that Graeme Sharp was coming through, made my decision for me. I went to Australia to play in the summer and I knew it was time for me to move on. Maybe if Howard had come in a couple of years earlier, I may have stayed at the club longer.'

But it was time for a new chapter. The 30-year - old made his debut for Swansea in the opening game of the 1981/82 season against Leeds United. In true Latchford style, he graced it with a hat-trick. And that was just the start as he kept up his remarkable goal-scoring record, powering the Swans to a creditable sixth in the League (having briefly topped the table earlier in the year).

The second season, however, was disastrous as financial difficulties beset the club. One by one, leading players left, with Latchford staying loyal as long as possible. His consolation goal at Old Trafford in May 1983 was to be Swansea's last in the top-flight for 28 years. Following relegation, he featured another 18 times before he too had to move on.

Over the next few seasons, with the years beginning to tell, he turned out for NAC Breda of Holland, Coventry City and Lincoln City before returning to South Wales for spells at Newport County and Merthyr Tydfil. It was at Merthyr that Latchford won his first bit of silverware when the non-league club were victorious in the 1987 Welsh FA Cup. He retired not long after, leaving football on a high, a fitting conclusion to a career that spanned 546 games and which had seen 231 goals.

Never keen on football management, Latchford went into business on retirement. He ran a children's clothes company and then a sports agency, before taking on a marketing role at Ladbrokes in the two years leading up to Euro 96.

This latter position led Latchford briefly back into football. His old Birmingham City teammate, Trevor Francis had become the club's manager and asked him to help establish the youth academy at St Andrews. There, they built it up from nothing, helping oversee the development of players, including future Everton forward, Andy Johnson.

After a few years with the youth set up, he eventually left Birmingham in 2001 to start a 'new life' in Austria with his new wife, Andrea. Today he is retired and lives in Germany, just one of the wide Blue diaspora that spans the globe.

Despite his Midlands roots and the varied football journey his career took, his heart remains at Everton. As he told James Corbett back in 2006 while working on his autobiography; 'I might have started at Birmingham, but my soul is at Goodison.'

GRAEME SHARP

(447 appearances, 159 goals)

'There was a perfect long ball played over the top by Gary Stevens,' recalls Graeme Sharp. 'My first touch was good, and I was aware that Mark Lawrenson was chasing. In a race, there was only going to be one winner and it wasn't me. So, with the ball bouncing nicely in front of me, I just thought, why not have a go? Fortunately for me, and the side, it flew in.'

There is a glorious photograph from the *Liverpool Echo* that captures that strike. In it, Sharp is in the air, having just unleashed his half-volley. Behind him, Mark Lawrenson watches, a slight look of apprehension on his face, as though at some level his brain has just begun to realise what is about to happen.

'A little Blue corner of the Kop exploded in response to Sharpe's volley sailing over Grobbelaar and into the back of the net' says Phil Redmond, co-founder of *When Skies Are Grey*, 'and what a way to go ahead in such a game. Our corner was rocking. It's the kind of goal you never forget. The moment it went in is seared into my memory.'

It was the moment that won the game, a victory that first suggested to the football world that Howard Kendall's young Everton side might have what it takes to go all the way. The goal gave Everton their first win at Anfield since 1970, an end to a 14-year drought.

During the 1970s and early 1980s, Everton had developed something of an inferiority complex in their attitude to the neighbours. The Derby, and particularly the Anfield fixture, had become a seasonal marker of the power balance in the city. It was as though until Everton could go there and win, the club would remain cowed, unable to break free from the neighbour's shadow.

Back in 1984, for the first time in a very long time, even amongst Evertonians, that most pessimistic of constituents, there was a feeling that this might, at last, be the time when the curse was lifted.

'We had gone to their place that day feeling more confident that we had for some time' explains John Flaherty. 'On the back of the FA Cup win in the May of that year, Everton had started the season brightly and for the first time in ages, we might have even been slight favourites going into that fixture.'

Certainly, they played like the favourites, confidently taking the game to Liverpool. But for all Everton's dominance, the goal would not come. What was needed was a moment of magic. And it arrived long after the break, courtesy of Everton's Scottish "Number 9".

'When you look back at that glory age in the mid-1980s' says Phil Redmond, 'certain goals always stand out; Steven's against Bayern, Gray in the FA Cup final against Watford, Inchy against Saints in the 84 FA semi-final. Sharp's is one of those. Not only was it a brilliant goal, but it also became an iconic strike because of what it represented. It meant that we had finally arrived.'

By that point, it had been four years since Sharp had come to Goodison, signed from Dumbarton by Gordon Lee in 1980.

He'd been born in Glasgow and had started his football journey playing for his local Boys Brigade team.

There's a great story from that time that gives an insight into Sharp's competitive and tenacious character. While playing for the Boys Brigade, his side found themselves 9-0 down and putting in a decidedly anaemic performance. Furious by his teammates' indifference to the ninth goal conceded, Sharp took the kick-off, dribbled through his own side and slammed in the tenth goal of the game through his own net, carrying on afterwards towards the changing rooms. For his efforts, he got a three-game suspension and time to reflect that there might be a better way to channel that competitive hunger.

From the Boys Brigade, he progressed to the school team and then onto Eastercraigs, one of the best amateur clubs around Glasgow. Modestly, Sharp had never considered himself anything special. And yet, as time passed, his obvious talents began to prick the interest of professional clubs and at the age of 17 he got picked up by Dumbarton.

At Boghead Park, Sharp developed into a promising young forward. Inevitably, he began to attract attention from south of the border, with several teams, including Notts County, Arsenal and Manchester United taking an interest in the young Scot.

Ironically, he also had two separate Andy Gray linked rumours during this time, once being considered by Aston Villa as a replacement for the recently sold Gray and then later looked at by Wolves as an understudy for his future teammate.

In the summer of 1980, despite being heavily linked with Villa again, and the club understanding that a deal was in the offing, Everton swooped in at the last minute and pipped their Midlands rivals to the signing.

It was one of those 'sliding doors' moments at Everton, as Gordon Lee, manager at the time revealed to *Lancashire Evening Post* in 2003:

'I remember at Everton I was looking for a second striker to play with Bob Latchford, and I went to watch Chester Reserves and a young boy called Ian Rush playing as an attacking midfielder. The next night, I was at Dumbarton and saw a raw striker called Graeme Sharp. I went back to the chairman and told him that, paired together, they could be one of the most exciting partnerships in English football. Chester wanted £300,000 for Rush, so I signed Graeme for £80,000 because the board said I couldn't have them both.'

But despite missing out on one of the great 'what if?' partnerships in English football, Everton had still landed a young player with enormous potential.

'And yet, early on, Sharp unquestionably struggled. In those early seasons, he only performed well in snatches,' recalls Phil Redmond. 'Although he clearly had talent, he seemed to find it hard to get into the rhythm of English football. It probably didn't help matters that under Lee and then early on under Kendall, the team wasn't playing well. It's always harder for younger players to break through into a side that struggles. It took quite a while to see the best of Sharpy.'

During the 1982/83 season, Sharp first began to give a hint of what was to come, finishing that campaign's top scorer with 15 league goals.

'There are some similarities with Dominic Calvert Lewin today' says lifelong Blue, Phil McMullen. 'Like him, Sharp was a young player who took his time to find his feet and then gradually started to build confidence and knowhow to become something a lot more threatening. They even play a similar way too. Great in the air, surprisingly deft with their feet and willing to run hard for the team, leading from the front.'

Even with his improved form, Sharp was still in a struggling side, something that didn't change until around a half-way through the 1983/84 campaign. Although the Scot put in plenty of hard work himself, he unquestionably benefited from wider changes affecting the team, including the promotion of the highly-rated youth-team coach, Colin Harvey, to the first team, the return to fitness and form of Peter Reid, and Neville Southall, recently returned from a spell on loan at Port Vale, beginning to show the keeping ability that he would go on to become famous for.

'It all combined to get the best out of Sharpy' recalls Andy Costigan of *Grand Old Team*. 'He became integral to those great sides of the mid-1980s. Sharpy was a playmaking centre-forward in my memory, tougher than he appeared and at times, unplayable in the air and no slouch with his feet too. He was a constant goal threat and I can only imagine opposition defenders had nightmares about playing against him. What Sharpy lacked in finesse he more than made up for with a dogged determination and his ability to lead the line with different players around him - he was adaptable.'

In the second half of the 1983/84 season, Everton's form improved massively, with only five defeats after the new year. It was a run that included appearances in both domestic cup finals. For Sharp, the FA Cup final against Watford, in particular, would prove to be a truly memorable day.

'Your first cup win always means the most. It's what you dream of when you start playing. And after the heartbreak of losing the League Cup final to Liverpool after a replay, the hunger for that trophy had only increased. To score the opening goal was a dream come true. I remember, the ball fell to Gary Stevens outside of the box and he had a go on goal. The shot was off target, but, luckily for me, the ball came my way about ten yards out. I was able to control it and put the ball past their keeper. I remember the Blue half of Wembley just exploding!'

Everton would end up 2-0 victors that day, bringing home the club's first piece of silverware since the 1970 league title. It was the kind of tangible success that laid the foundations for what was to come.

'Once you've won one trophy then you start to get

the hunger for more. And with the players we had in that team, and the management, the tools were there to do something about it' says Sharp.

In the season that followed, one in which Everton were imperious, Sharp led the line impeccably, scoring 30 goals in 55 appearances across all competitions.

'He was consistently good' says Phil Redmond. 'First with Heath as his partner up front and then after Inchy got injured, with Andy Gray, he adapted his game accordingly, always working hard for the team and providing important goals.'

Goals, such as that one at Anfield. Although, as impressive as it was, according to Sharp, he cannot take all the credit for the strike: 'Liverpool used to use Adidas Tango balls in their games. So, the week before, Howard had us training with them. And I think that little bit of practice gave me a feel for them and helped with the goal. I might not have struck the ball so cleanly without that little bit of forethought from Howard.'

It was a goal that lit the touch-paper for a memorable season, one that would end with the title and the Cup Winners Cup.

'That was a fantastic side' Sharp recalls. 'Although we all had talent and we had a great set up with Howard and Colin, it also helped that we got on with each other on and off the pitch. There was a great camaraderie in the dressing room. So, you had a group of players, [including those who didn't always feature in the starting eleven] who wanted to fight for each other and fight for the shirt. And when you have that, combined with quality, then you are always in with a chance.'

As great as those sides of the mid-1980s were at gathering trophies, they were very nearly so much better. In the 1984/5 season, the club just missed out on a historic treble after losing the FA Cup final to Manchester United. In the following season, this time with Gary Lineker partnering Sharp up-front, the club was pipped to the double by Liverpool.

'That side, with Sharp and Lineker up front was one of the great Everton teams. In any other season, it would've brought home silverware. I remember at the time that most people in the game thought we were the better team and Liverpool had been lucky to get the better of us twice. And although Lineker tended to generate the headlines, because he scored so freely, you can't ignore Sharp's contribution. Not only did he contribute with goals of his own, but he also worked so hard for the team. I think when you have a front pairing that score over 60 goals between them over the season, in the league and the cups, you can see what a great partnership that was' says Phil

McMullen.

Regardless of the great football on offer, that was a frustrating time to be an Evertonian. Not only had one of the club's greatest sides been denied the opportunity to compete in Europe (following the post-Heysel ban) but it had watched on helplessly as its nearest rival brought home the trophies that could, and possibly should, have been Everton's.

'And so, after those near misses, and the frustration felt by the fans after the ban, in the 1986/7 season we were really fired up to claim some more silverware' remembers Sharp.

Despite the quality in the team, it would end up proving to be a much tougher prospect for Everton than in recent seasons. Not only had Lineker parted company with the club, sold to Barcelona in the summer, the squad was also blighted by injuries all season.

'It might not have been as swashbuckling as 1984/85, but in some ways, the 1986/87 title win was more impressive. Against the odds and often with a patched-up side, we triumphed' remembers Sharp.

'A squad effort is harder to pull off' he continues 'And so, the way that Howard brought players in and chopped and changed the side in response to adversity just showed what a great manager he was.'

But he was also a manager about to sever his links with the club (for the time being at least). That title win proved to be the swansong of the Ken- dall-era Mark I. The desire to manage a side capable of playing in Europe forced him to look elsewhere, ultimately meaning a move to Athletic Bilbao in Spain.

In his place, the first-team coach, Colin Harvey, came in to take charge of the reigns. For Everton, and Sharp, things were never as great again. The loss of Kendall set in motion a slow decline at Goodison as the club struggled with the transition. Not only did the new players brought in often not meet the stand- ard of the great sides of the mid-1980s, but Harvey also found it difficult to bring unity to the squad. In the end, he found himself ruling over two camps, one made up of the new arrivals and the other the Kendall old-guard. Inevitably it was not a recipe for success.

Although under Harvey, Sharp's contribution each season started to gradually decline, he still had it in him to bring moments of magic to Everton's games, as Andy Costigan recalls:

'One abiding memory of Sharpy came on a freezing cold November game at Fratton Park against Alan Balls' Portsmouth. It was absolutely bitter and a dour, dour game that saw seven yellow cards and two red, both for Pompey, with the only illuminating moment coming late in the game. Sharpy struck a volley of venomous power from just outside the box that flew into the top corner like an Exocet missile. The Anfield volley gets all the plaudits, but that Fratton Park effort was every bit as good and made that long journey all the more worthwhile.'

But over time, even the moments of magic began to dry up. By the time Harvey was sacked in 1990, replaced by a returning Kendall, the once towering Scot, now pushing 30, was not the force he had been.

'Sharp, in particular, is the picture of what is wrong with Everton,' wrote Dave Jones in *When Skies Are Grey*. 'The way he ambles across the pitch, doing practically nothing all game, and he still gets picked every week.'

Although he was widely regarded as one of the club's great centre-forwards, when Sharp was sold to Oldham Athletic for £500,000 in 1991, most Blues saw it as decent business. And it turned out a good move for all parties involved. In his first season at Boundary Park, Sharpe's 12 league goals enabled Oldham to survive the 1991/92 campaign, meaning that they would be members of the new Premier League. In the following season, his goals once again helped them avoid relegation, this time on goal difference.

When Latics boss, Joe Royle quit as Oldham manager to come to Everton in November 1994, Sharp took over as player-manager, guiding the club to a mid-table finish in the second tier (they had been relegated a season earlier). It was a disappointing showing for a side who had retained all but one of their key players. Further disappointment came in 1995/96 when Oldham finished 18th. Under pressure, Sharp finally walked in March of 1997 with Oldham on the verge of relegation to the third tier.

After Boundary Park, the Scot enjoyed a brief dalliance as manager of Bangor City in the League of Wales for one season, where he led the club to a Welsh Cup victory in May 1998. It was a win that brought a close to his managerial career. Since then he has come back to Goodison, working as a club ambassador and now as the club's first 'Players' Life President'.

'He's one of those figures who has become synonymous with the club' says John Daley. 'He's effectively given most of his life to Everton, both professionally and after retirement from the game. But as valuable as his work is off the pitch, we'll always love him most for what he did on it. He led the line during the Golden Age. And he scored massively important goals. I think I'll always picture him mid-volley against the Shite at their place in '84, hitting that exquisite volley over the head of a despairing Grobbelaar. What a way to be remembered.'

ANDY GRAY

(68 appearances, 22 goals)

When Andy Gray came to Goodison in November 1983, the move represented something of a last throw of the dice for both the player and the club.

Everton under Kendall were in a dire position. 'There had been hints that Kendall was on to something in his first few seasons, but we'd then started the 83/84 campaign really poorly,' remembers, Phil Redmond. 'I'm not one to get into all that "sack the manager" stuff, but even I joined in with calls for him to go during an away game against Leicester in October when we'd just been shite. He'd had a few seasons and we were getting the sense as fans that he just didn't have what it would take to get Everton up to where we wanted them to be.'

Goals, in particular, had been hard to come by. By early November, the team had managed just seven in the league. With Graeme Sharp struggling temporarily with injuries, confidence and form, his comrades in the Everton front line were doing little to share the burden: David Johnson had a single league goal to his name, Adrian Heath not one.

The man that Kendall turned to as a remedy to this problem did not come risk-free. By 1983, Andy Gray was widely thought to not be the player he once was.

Born in Glasgow, Gray, for a time, had been the hottest property in British football. The Scot, who received his footballing education at Drumchapel Amateurs in Glasgow – the club who could boast Alex Ferguson, David Moyes, John Wark, John Robertson and Alan Brazil as alumni– had started his professional career playing for Dundee United in 1973, scoring freely at Tannadice before pricking the interest of clubs in England.

In October 1975, Aston Villa succeeded in obtaining his signature, shelling out £110,000 for the young Scot. And it was money well spent. The following season he scored 29 goals and earned both the PFA Young Player of the Year award and the PFA Player of the Year Award - a double achievement only repeated since by Cristiano Ronaldo and Gareth Bale.

Despite his value to the side, in a surprise move, he was sold to local rivals Wolves for a British record £1.5m in 1979. The Molineux club, hoping to recapture past glories, placed their hopes on the shoulders of Gray.

Although he scored the winning goal in the League Cup final during his first season with Wolves, Gray's time at Molineux was blighted by both the team's rapid deterioration and, more significantly, by his recurrent injury problems. By November 1983, his troublesome knees had become his defining characteristic. Wolves, who were in the midst of a death-spiral down the divisions in a whirlwind of debt, increasingly saw the sale of the unreliable Scot as a relatively risk-free way to help stave off the threat of going out of business.

And that's where Kendall's gambit came in. With a limited budget, just £250,000, he hoped the 28-year-old Gray might represent a cut-price answer to his prayers.

But the move did not, initially, go down well with Evertonians.

The *Football Echo* letters pages were deluged with complaints, missives accusing Everton of buying another knackered veteran, there for payday (to add to Peter Reid). Understandably, this was not how Gray viewed the move:

'I knew the responsibility that was on my shoulders' he recalls. 'When you come to a club like Everton and you wear that "Number 9" shirt, you know what's expected of you. I came to the club to do my best for it and to win things. I still had something to prove in the game and I saw the move as a great opportunity.'

If the under-fire Everton manager expected an immediate impact from his new acquisition, a contribution to quell the misgivings of the fans, he was to be sorely disappointed. Indeed, so impotent was Gray, that Kendall dropped him after a few games, sparking a disagreement between the pair which almost saw the Scot leave the club not long after the ink on his contract had dried.

And yet, despite the brief falling out, Gray remained. Which was just as well for Everton because even if he wasn't contributing on the pitch, at least behind the scenes, on the training ground, his natural charisma and winning mentality were starting to make an impact on a squad devoid of self-belief.

When he had first arrived at the club, in his first press conference, Gray had already provided a taste of what he brought to the table. The assembled hacks had asked the new arrival why he had come to Everton. 'To win things,' was his response. When they pointed out that many others in his position had said exactly the same thing, he replied, 'You've never heard it from me.'

It was the kind of self-assurance that Everton's young squad lacked.

'Adrian Heath told me he and the other young players would look at Andy Gray – and Peter Reid too – and get a lesson in what it took to win football matches. Including the nasty stuff, as we saw in that Bayern Munich semi at Goodison when he broke a defender's nose. What stands out for me is the Cup final Grandstand clip of Reid and Gray on the Everton bus en route to Wembley in 1984 as it brings home Gray's sheer force of personality. His charisma jumps out of the screen' says Simon Hart.

Around the turn of the year, something, at last, began to click amongst Kendall's young team, as that 'blend of youth and experience' finally started to gel. Gray's form, which also began to improve, added to this, providing Kendall's young side with a sense of steely determination.

'There were a few games in January - Birmingham away in the league, Stoke away in the FA Cup, Oxford United away in the League Cup - when you got the first signs that things were starting to go our way' remembers Gray. 'People have their own opinion about which game was the most important. But, whichever one you go for, it soon became clear that this side, which until recently had been thought of as relegation candidates, suddenly had something about them.'

The two cup runs that season, first the League Cup and then the FA did a lot to galvanise the squad, instilling a sense of confidence and belief that had been sorely lacking. In the FA Cup, Gray played his part, opening the scoring with a stupendous header against Stoke in the third round, bagging an implausible header against Notts County in the quarter-finals - diving at a ball just six inches off the ground-

and, of course, scoring the second goal in the final against Watford.

'That was an amazing moment' he recalls. 'I'd dreamed of scoring in an FA Cup final as a kid, so to actually do it and go on to win the trophy was wonderful. I know it wasn't the prettiest of goals but they all count. It capped what was a great day for us and the fans. It had been a long time since Everton had won any silverware and after the disappointment of losing the League Cup, we felt we owed it to the fans to bring this one home.'

On the back of that victory, Everton went into the following season with a rare sense of confidence, with there even being whispers of a possible title challenge.

'And it was easy to see why' says Gray. 'We'd played exceptionally well during the second half of the previous season. We were united as a group of players, with that vital sense of togetherness. But perhaps more important than anything else, we'd tasted success. Not only did that FA Cup final show us and the football world that we had what it took to win silverware, it also made us hungry for more.'

But, to begin with at least, Gray was a marginal presence in the side. Injuries and the blossoming of the Sharpe/Heath strike partnership meant that he didn't feature much during the early part of the season. But that was to change in December. After months of waiting, Gray finally got his opportunity to cement a place in the side. Although it was an opportunity that arose in the bleakest of circumstances, the horrific injury sustained by Adrian Heath during a home game against Sheffield Wednesday in December.

'At that time, Inchy and Sharpy were probably the best strike partnerships in England, if not Europe. They had been a key reason why we were thought of as genuine title contenders. So, when it happened, there were obviously thoughts amongst the fans that this could hurt us. It probably didn't help that I was not a like-for-like replacement. Sharpy and I were similar players, so it would have been understandable for people to wonder how playing together was going to work. But we were mates, we understood each other and we're intelligent footballers. We made sure that it worked and that the side's momentum kept going' says Gray.

From the 1st of December to the 11th of May, Gray played his part in an Everton team which only lost one league game, scoring eight important goals in the process. Two performances from this period stand out. In a vital 2-1 away win at Leicester City in February, the Scot showed his tenacity by almost knocking himself unconscious as he collided with a goalpost heading in Everton's opener. Later in the season, against Sunderland at Goodison, Gray scored two majestic diving headers, delivering a master-class in footballing aerial ability in the midst of what was one of the side's most accomplished performances of the season.

The title, which had increasingly possessed an air of inevitably about it, was eventually sewn up at home against QPR with five games left to spare; the Blues ending the season 13 points ahead of nearest rivals Liverpool. For many Evertonians, Gray's contribution that season had been invaluable.

'He was all action, selfless and utterly fearless. At times, his centre-forward play bordered on being foolhardy, but his sheer grit and determination pulled all the other players together into an even more cohesive and effective force. Gray, for me, was the catalyst that transformed a more than capable side into a side who had all the hallmarks of being serial winners' says Andy Costigan.

As important as Gray had been in the hunt for the title, some of his best performances that season occurred in the European Cup Winners Cup. He scored his first ever Everton hat trick as the Blues beat Fortuna Sittard 3-0 in the quarter-final. And then came the legendary second leg of the semi-final against Bayern Munich at Goodison, a game that has since become indelibly etched within Everton folklore.

The first leg, played in the Olympiastadion München, had been a tough game for the Blues. With a slightly patched-up side, they ground out a 0–0 draw, giving them a theoretical advantage in the tie.

'But despite that, and the fact that we were playing well and on course to win the title, nobody gave us a prayer and it was understandable why' says Gray. 'This was the mighty Bayern Munich playing against a bunch of kids and a few old pros like me and Reidy. We were a bit of an unknown quantity I suppose, and so the question for those watching was probably whether we would rise to the occasion or buckle in the face of a more experienced opponent?'

On a balmy night in April, the moment of truth arrived. 'The atmosphere that night was incredible,' remembers Graham Ennis, former editor of *When Skies Are Grey*. 'The place was heaving and the noise was breath-taking. You have to remember that there were only about 50 Bayern supporters there. We had 50,000 Blues, under the lights and completely behind the side.'

In the first half, Everton were unquestionably the better side. But, despite their dominance, clear-cut chances were limited. Sheedy came close with a free-kick, Sharp with a header, and there was also a decent penalty shout when the ball appeared to strike the arm of Dremmler in the box.

'I don't think Bayern knew what hit them,' says Gray. 'Compared to other performances that season, we weren't playing with the same degree of fluidity. Instead, physicality was given more emphasis. That was the game plan and it worked. Bayern looked rattled.'

And yet, despite Everton's physically domineering approach, it would be the Bavarians who would take the lead, through Hoeness.

'The moment that ball went in it was like someone had deflated a balloon,' Gray recalls. 'Just for a second, all the life was sucked out of Goodison. But, to the credit of the fans, it didn't last long. Within moments, they were up again, willing us on to get an equaliser.'

Although the Blues went into the break 1-0 down, within minutes of the start, they were back in the game when Sharp equalized.

The atmosphere, which had been electric all night, appeared to become even more charged. According to Gray, when added to Everton's physical approach, it tipped the balance in their favour.

'I'd not heard a noise like that crowd. And you could see that Bayern were suffering. It was intense. And they were also finding our physicality harder and harder to cope with. When you saw their players lying down on the pitch whingeing about a particularly tenacious tackle, then psychologically you knew we'd got the better of them. And that was a hugely important part of the battle.'

For the next 20 minutes, the Blues hustled and bustled, creating a few decent chances and barely letting the Bavarians get their foot on the ball. Even though at 1–1 Bayern were still in the stronger position, it only ever felt like one team would emerge victorious and that it was a case of when rather than if another Everton goal would come. When it did, with 15 minutes left, it arrived courtesy of Gray:

'Another huge throw-in from Gary Stevens came into the box,' Gray recalls, 'where the Bayern keeper and a few defenders managed to miss the ball, which then fell perfectly for me to sweep it into the net. I remember the noise from the Gwladys Street almost hitting me when the ball crossed the line.'

Trevor Steven's goal a few minutes from the end merely confirmed what everyone watching already knew, that Everton had booked a place in the final.

And there they would meet Rapid Vienna, an opponent that held little fear for a confident Everton.

'We knew in our hearts that we would beat them' says Gray. 'A few of us, Reidy, Inchy and Sharpy and I, had gone to watch one of their games earlier in the competition in Manchester. We all agreed that there had been nothing in that performance to give us any reason to fear them. We knew we were by far the better side.'

And so it proved to be. In a one-sided game in Rotterdam, Everton were dominant. In the end, the final score-line of 3-1 flattered the Austrians, who had been so far off Everton's pace that it was a wonder how they had managed to get that far.

'I got our first in that game' Gray recalls. 'I had an open goal and just volleyed the ball into the net. It was an incredible feeling. And it was the goal that killed the match in my opinion. Our opponents had shown little before that, and after we scored, you got the sense that they had nothing to offer.'

Despite narrowly missing out on the Treble after losing to Manchester United in the FA Cup final a few days later, Everton and Gray could still look back on the season with considerable satisfaction. The gamble that had represented his move had paid off better than anyone could have expected, a move that had revitalised both parties.

But football can be a cruel game. Still on a high from a season few had seen coming, playing the best football he had for some time and assured by Howard Kendall that he formed a key part of his plans for the forthcoming campaign, Gray moved to a new house in Formby.

Not long after, just as he was about to go on holiday to Portugal, his manager turned up to deliver some devastating news, informing him that he intended to buy Gary Lineker from Leicester City and that, should he be interested, Aston Villa wanted to buy him back. Believing that the arrival spelled the end of his Everton career, Gray accepted the move. It was a decision, as he recently revealed to *Toffee TV,* that he came to regret:

'Hindsight is a wonderful thing...and I think if I would have taken more time to think about it, to absorb what Howard had said to me, I think I would have stayed. But I was so upset, so disappointed, when Howard said he was going to sign Gary and that I wouldn't be playing at the beginning of the season.'

The absence of European football, denied the club following the Heysel ban, also, according to Gray, played its part.

'Staying [at Everton] would have been too good an opportunity to have missed. To play in a European Cup campaign. I think it would have been difficult to have walked away from that. 100 per cent difficult. Even though Gary came in, I still think that having been part of the team that had got us the title, and got us into the European Cup, had we been there, that would have been hard to walk away from.'

Understandably, the move, and specifically Kendall's apparent decision to marginalise a crowd favourite, caused outrage amongst Blues. Petitions were drawn up and fans in their thousands wrote to the club demanding that Gray should remain an Everton player.

But nothing would change the outcome and so Gray returned to the Midlands. There he found a very different Aston Villa to the club he had left. The days of eying the top of the table had receded, with Villa now more focused on trying to avoid relegation. In his first season back, Gray managed just five goals from 35 league games as Villa narrowly avoided relegation to the Second Division. That meagre return looked positively bountiful during his second campaign at Villa Park, with Gray failing to score a single goal from the 19 league games he featured in. It was a season that would conclude with Villa succumbing to the drop.

From there he moved west (slightly), spending a fruitless season with West Brom before heading north to Scotland, joining Rangers in the summer of 1988. At Ibrox, he helped the 'Gers' to the first of nine successive titles they would win, before moving on once again after a single campaign, ending his career at Cheltenham Town in the Football Conference.

After his playing days were over, Gray went quickly into commentary with Sky, where he forged a career for himself. Although settled there, he was very nearly tempted to break ranks on one occasion and try his hand at management. In the summer of 1997, Everton were in the hunt for a new boss following the end of Joe Royle's tenure in charge. Gray interviewed for the position, was offered it and seemed to be on the cusp of accepting. But, at the last minute he had a change of heart, even the lure of his beloved Goodison not proving strong enough to make him shift careers.

And that meant there would be no managerial odyssey to potentially taint the legacy, leaving Evertonians instead with the memories of his glorious spell as player. They were nineteen months that helped create the club's Golden Age. Like all success, it was a team effort. But the impact of the Scot with the brittle knees cannot be underestimated. Perhaps not since Dean, had a single player changed the footballing fortunes of an Everton team so dramatically. He might not have been as prolific as his great forbear, but Andrew Mullen Gray was just as transformative, a signing that acted as the catalyst; that alchemical element to help create the greatest Everton side to ever play at Goodison.

DUNCAN FERGUSON

(273 appearances, 72 goals)

It's difficult to imagine a time when 'Big Dunc' conjured up little more than indifference amongst Evertonians. It's almost as though you can divide Everton chronology into the era that existed Before Duncan (B.D.) and that which has existed after Duncan (A.D). But before he became a legend, he was just a player. And at first, not a great one.

According to Alan Pattullo, author of *In Search of Duncan Ferguson: The Life and Crimes of a Footballing Enigma*, his journey to Goodison arose quite by accident:

'Peter Johnson, and some other members of the board had travelled to Rangers, Ferguson's club at the time, to investigate ways to increase hospitality streams. Whilst there, they met up with Rangers' manager Walter Smith and talk moved on to players.'

At this point, Everton, still under the woeful stewardship of Mike Walker, were without a win in the league and Johnson saw this as an opportunity to bring some much-needed fresh blood to the squad.

'Initially' continues Pattullo, 'the aim was to bring the midfielders Ian Durrant and Trevor Steven in on a permanent deal. But as Everton were in need of some additional fire-power, they also inquired after Mark Hateley. With the striker not keen on a move south,

Ferguson was offered to the club instead.'

In the end, Steven's move fell through and Everton ended up taking Durrant on loan for a month and Ferguson for three.

'The only reason Duncan came on loan [and not bought]' Mike Walker told Pattullo when interviewed for his book 'was because the chairman was a bit unsure, telling me that "I don't know about this, he's a bad lad". We didn't have limitless pots of money, which didn't help either. Basically, I said "why don't we get him on loan? If we get him on loan we win two ways - we get a look at the lad, and if he is a real hot head then we can let him go. Let's take him - see what he's like?" Let's give him the chance I thought.'

Far from being greeted as a transfer coup, the deals were met with derision by the media, with headlines such as 'Farce', 'Walkers Wobbles' and 'Loan Rangers Fiasco' appearing in the national press.

The negative reaction was a response to the baggage that both players brought with them. Durrant had suffered a career-threatening knee injury that had left him out of competitive football for almost three years. It led inevitably to question marks about his fitness. And in Ferguson, it was a measure of Everton's desperation over the side's lack of potency up front that the club had turned to a player who'd developed a reputation for being ill-disciplined and whose form had declined markedly.

Despite his abundant promise, the Scot had endured a difficult time since his £4m move from Dundee United to Rangers in the summer of 1993. Ferguson had only put in 14 appearances for the Old Firm giant and scored just two goals. He'd also fallen foul of both the football and the legal authorities following an on-the-pitch altercation during which he had head-butted John McStay of Raith Rovers. The incident would earn Ferguson a 12-game ban from the Scottish FA and attract the attention of the Procurator Fiscal, who for the first time in Scottish legal history would prosecute a footballer for assault on the field of play.

Expensive to keep, off form and a source of controversy, according to Pattullo, Rangers appeared content to farm out their troubled forward for a time.

'Since his altercation with McStay in April 1994, Ferguson had largely become a fixture on the bench. Back then, the club had the good fortune that Mark Hateley, the man Ferguson had been bought to replace, had been playing well, so there was less need for Dunc to be part of the club [or on the wage bill].'

For Everton and Walker, the hope was that a change of scene would do the Scot some good, enabling him to recapture the form that he displayed at Dundee

United. But during Ferguson's early days at Goodison, this looked like wishful thinking.

'There was little in the Scot's performances to suggest that his loan period would ever be extended. He looked listless, uninterested and nothing like the player he'd been at Dundee United. Any hopes that the introduction of a supposedly talented "Number 9" would transform our season had been quashed. Ferguson didn't inspire hope in the slightest' remembers Neil Roberts, author of *Blues & Beatles: Football, Family and the Fab Four - the Life of an Everton Supporter*.

Considering the degree of reverence that still surrounds Ferguson, it was Durrant who was received with more affection by the fans to begin with. Not only had he bothered to attend his first press conference in the correctly coloured attire (Ferguson opted for an inflammatory red blazer), he also appeared more committed on the pitch.

'I don't think Ferguson took the loan seriously early on. You have to appreciate that his move to Rangers, his boyhood club, had been a dream come true. That's where his heart lay. His time in Liverpool probably felt temporary. At this point, Ferguson was a player who likely thought that playing for Everton was a step down for him and that the sooner he could get back up north the better' thinks Pattullo.

Early on into his loan period, the manager who brought Ferguson to Goodison was sacked. Walker, who had led Everton to a dismal start to the campaign, was replaced by Joe Royle. Immediately, Royle began to create a very different kind of Everton, a shift from the anaemic, possession football of Walker to something tougher and more direct. In theory, it was a style of play better suited to the Scot. But only time would tell if he would respond.

The first test for both the players and the new approach was Liverpool at home. It was a game when the fans first got to see the 'Dogs of War' in action, Royle's tenacious midfield of Parkinson, Ebbrell and Horne. They harried and chased Liverpool all night, refusing to give them time to breathe. And it was also the first time that the supporters got to see a very different kind of Duncan Ferguson, the player who would become talismanic for the Blues in the mid-1990s.

If one moment could be said to have changed the Scot's reputation at Goodison it would be the goals scored that night. Stan Osborne takes up the story:

'It was in the second half. We'd controlled Liverpool but as yet, not created too many chances. We'd looked most dangerous from Andy Hinchliffe's precision-guided corners, which had been causing Liverpool problems all night but without yielding anything for the home side. That was about to change. Around the 50-minute mark, Ferguson connected with one and put the ball narrowly over the bar. It was a warning shot to Liverpool, one that to their cost they failed to heed. When Ferguson met the next corner, he didn't head the ball, he butted it. There was a moment, just as the ball crossed the line but before it hit the back of the net when Goodison was silent. Then, when we all realised what had happened there was just an explosion of noise.'

Everton would go on to win the game 2-0. Not only had they defeated the auld enemy but the three points represented a vital first step in the club's fight to avoid relegation.

'It was an incredible night' remembers Graham Ennis. 'Nobody had given us a chance before the game, so to get the win was amazing. And that, plus great performances in the weeks that followed, finally gave us some hope. This new version of Everton under Royle looked tenacious, the kind of side who knew what it took to get out of the bottom three. And in Ferguson, an old-fashioned centre forward, like a great Everton "Number 9" from the club's past, we seemed to have a strong presence to build everything around. One of my greatest memories of that night, and that season, was being on County Road after the Derby, waiting to get a bus into town and seeing Ferguson strutting down the road like he was the king of the city.'

Although he was never a prolific scorer and could be anonymous against the smaller clubs, 'Big Dunc' became the totemic embodiment of Everton's revival during the remainder of that campaign.

'It was a pretty grey time being an Evertonian in the early 90s – we were a team and a club in decline. In the Kendall Mark-II-era, we had had that team of midgets – Beardsley, Cottee, Ward. Some nice footballers but suddenly, here was this formidable "Number 9" in an Everton shirt again. Moreover, he brought the fear factor. He had an arrogance that really came through in the big matches – just look at all the goals he scored against Liverpool and Man United. People were laughing at Everton when Mike Walker was manager. Joe Royle changed that, with the help of some very good footballers. But it was Duncan who was the talismanic figure the fans latched on to' says Simon Hart.

The season's narrative unquestionably helped Ferguson. Not only did Royle manage to engineer a miraculous survival in the league, the club ended the campaign as FA Cup winners. A bleaker outcome might've soured how that side was viewed and the way in which the players connected to the crowd. As it was, Blues could end the season on a high, revelling in the imagery of the iconic Scot holding the cup aloft.

But although Ferguson brought much to the side, he also came with baggage, and in the following campaign the fans got to experience the impact this could have. To begin with, he missed most of the early part of the season due to injury.

'That was something that plagued his career' says Phil McMullen. 'Whenever he seemed to be finding form, suddenly he'd get another injury. It might have just been the way he played. Dunc threw himself into everything and inevitably, I suppose, that comes with risks. But after we signed him permanently, for around £4.5m, it was something we had to put up with. He was a player we had to have but also one that, disappointingly, we spent too much time without.'

Allied to an unenviable injury record, Ferguson also suffered from disciplinary problems throughout his career. And in his first full season with the club, Everton were on the receiving end of this issue at its most extreme. Just as the Scot was beginning to return to full fitness after his lay off, he was forced to go north for the culmination of his long-running dispute with the Scottish legal system.

The case against Ferguson had been tried in the week following the FA Cup Final and had gone against him. He was found guilty of assault and sentenced to three months in prison. Sheriff Alexander Eccles had told the Glasgow Sheriff Court that Ferguson needed to be jailed 'in the public interest' to illustrate to the wider country that such behaviour would not be tolerated, something that would be assisted by Ferguson's position as a high-profile footballer.

Although he appealed, it was to no avail. In early October, Lord Hope, the Lord Justice General of Scotland upheld the sentence. Ferguson would be taken to Glasgow's Barlinnie Prison to serve his time, the first British footballer to be jailed for an on-field offence.

'That might've been an extreme example of his tendency to get into trouble, but it was indicative of a player who often let his temper get the better of himself during his career. It felt like because of suspensions and injuries, we only ever got to see a fraction of what Ferguson could have been' thinks Phil Redmond.

Ferguson did eventually return to the fold. The Scot's sentence was cut short and he was released in late November. Not long after, 11,000 Blues attended to watch him turn-out for a reserve game against Newcastle. At the time, he was ineligible to play for the first team because the Scottish FA's 12 game ban was in force.

Following a challenge by the club, who claimed that their player was being punished twice for the same offence, the ban was eventually overturned by a judicial review. Ferguson returned to the senior fray for a home game against Wimbledon on New Year's Day 1996, scoring twice in a 3-2 win.

And for the next few seasons, he carried on from where he had left off; missing some games, turning up for others, scoring the occasional memorable goal. Although he never quite recaptured the magic of that first campaign, while fit and free from suspension, he remained a figure held in great affection.

'You always felt that Dunc understood what it was to be an Evertonian, that he "got" the club. And no matter whether it was the good times, like winning the FA Cup, or the bad times, like nearly going down against Coventry, he cared about what was happening just as much as you did. And I think it was this sense that he was one of our own that made the decision to sell him to Newcastle in 1998 so shocking to the fans' says Phil McMullen.

Sold for £8m without his knowledge, or the knowledge of Walter Smith, the manager at the time, it was a move that had nothing to do with football and everything to do with the bottom line.

'Everton needed the money' says Dave Prentice. 'Contrary to what the supporters assumed, that the summer spending on the likes of John Collins and Olivier Dacourt had come from fresh investment, in reality,

Peter Johnson had simply extended the club's over-draft. The club was in debt and as one of its leading assets, the sale of Ferguson could help plug that.'

The move, briefly, threw the club into crisis. Smith threatened to resign and the fans were in open revolt. Ferguson himself inflamed the situation when he let it be known in *The Evertonian*, how against the move he had been:

'I was numb with shock really. It sickened me' he said 'I couldn't believe it. I am absolutely heartbroken to leave the club. I think everyone knows what Everton Football Club means to me. I thought I would finish my career there and I wanted to finish my career at Goodison Park. I approached the club for the new contract which I signed last season and a month ago I had been talking to my agent about asking for an extension to that deal. I was happy to be at Everton for life, if they wanted me. In the last couple of days my world has turned upside down.'

Although all parties settled down, the sale was the final nail in the coffin for the reign of owner, Peter Johnson. His stock already low following the club's continued decline (and near-death experience during the 1997/98 season), the sale of the club's most popular player proved to be a blow he could not recover from. Within 18 months, the club had been sold and with that, the Johnson-era was brought to a close.

But the Ferguson-era at Everton was not yet over. Although he spent nearly two years at St James' Park, continued injuries meant he barely featured for the first team. By the summer of 2000, Newcastle were looking to off-load him and Everton came calling, bringing the forward back home for £3.75m.

During his first game back at Goodison, the returning hero came on with 25 minutes to go, scoring two in a 3–0 win over Charlton. But if Evertonians were hoping that it was a taste of things to come, they were to be disappointed (for a few seasons at least).

'I remember being at Goodison to lap up the excitement of his first game back in 2000 but during that second spell, with the injuries and occasional rushes of blood to the head, it felt he'd become an expensive luxury the club could barely afford. Think of the time he grabbed Steffen Freund around the throat at Leicester. But, thankfully, during the 2004/05 campaign, some of the old magic came back and Dunc scored some big goals which helped us finish fourth and qualify for the Champions League. Winning goals against Norwich and Fulham and of course the glorious header against Man United' says Simon Hart.

The following campaign, 2005/06, would prove to be Ferguson's swansong. Pretty much consigned to life as a support player, the Scot would only score once all season, and that would be in his final game. It came on 7 May 2006, against West Brom at Goodison. Making a rare start, Ferguson was named captain. If the fans watching were keen to see their idol end his Blue career on a high, they had a long wait. In the 90th-minute, Mikel Arteta won Everton a penalty. There was only one person to take it. Ferguson stepped up. In truth, it was a poor strike, easy for the keeper to save. But luck was on the Scot's side. The ball rebounded kindly, allowing him to smash it into the back of the net, securing his final goal for the club at the Gwladys Street, the same end where he had scored his first.

'It brought to a close, from a playing perspective, one of the most memorable Everton careers in the modern age' says Phil McMullen. 'If you just looked at the stats alone, you wouldn't think that Ferguson was much of a player. But he was about so much more than that. When he announced his arrival in that Derby game back in 1994, he gave the fans something that they had been missing for a long time, a genuine hero. And that mattered. Times were tough for us in the 1990s and we needed someone like Big Dunc to believe in. And whenever he played, even during that second spell when he'd lost a bit of the old magic, you knew he'd die for the club.'

Of course, the end of his playing days did not mean that Ferguson's relationship with the club had been brought to a conclusion. After five years out of the game, he returned to Everton in 2011, invited by David Moyes to become part of the youth set-up. Since then, he has advanced to the first team coaching staff and during the club's recent merry-go-round of managerial appointments has remained a rare constant.

He even had a crack at the top job, stepping into the caretaker's role upon the sacking of Marco Silva in December 2019. With Everton residing in the bottom three at the time and facing a tough run of fixtures, there were parallels with that bleak time in 1994 when he had first come to the club. But, as he did back then, Ferguson rose to the challenge. Starting with a home win over Chelsea, his version of Everton, tougher, more direct and harder to break down, hauled themselves out of the danger zone, turning around a season that had threatened to career out of control.

As he ran along the touchline after the first goal against Chelsea, fists held aloft, it was as though the years had been rolled back. Big Dunc, the 'King of the City', back doing what he did best.

Printed in Great Britain
by Amazon

49867566R00083